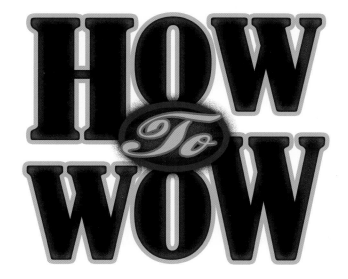

HOW TO WOW

With Photoshop Elements 5

Jack Davis · Mike McHugh · Wayne Rankin
with Brie Gyncild

Peachpit Press

How to Wow with Photoshop Elements 5
Jack Davis, Mike McHugh, and Wayne Rankin

Peachpit Press
1249 Eighth Street
Berkeley, CA 94710
(510) 524-2178
(510) 524-2221 (fax)
Find us on the Web at www.peachpit.com.
To report errors, please send a note to errata@peachpit.com.

Peachpit Press is a division of Pearson Education.
Copyright © 2007 by Jack Davis, Mike McHugh, and Wayne Rankin

Editor: Rebecca Gulick
Writer: Brie Gyncild
Production Coordinator: David Van Ness
Technical Editors: Jack Davis, Mike McHugh, and Wayne Rankin
Compositor: Mike McHugh
Indexer: Karin Arrigoni
Proofreader: Liz Welch
Cover Design: Jack Davis
Interior Design: Jill Davis

ISBN 0-321-48615-3
9 8 7 6 5 4 3 2 1

Printed and bound in the United States of America

Acknowledgments

First of all, I would like to thank Jack Davis. If it were not for a chance meeting in 1989 at Macworld Sydney, I would not have had the opportunity to know this great person, wonderful designer, photographer, digital master, father, and surfer. (He makes big waves wherever he goes.) That relationship now culminates in my being involved in the exciting new "How to Wow" series of books. Good onya, Mate!

Of course there is the beautiful Jill, his partner in life, and a truly talented person as well. Jill, thanks for your wisdom, guidance, and direction during the production of this book.

Then there's Mike McHugh, my partner in crime (coauthor). We both live in a beautiful part of Australia, in the town of Warrandyte. Mike is recognized as one of the most experienced teachers in Australia for Adobe software.

To Patrick Lorr at iStockphoto.com, who gave us access to an extensive and wonderfully rich online image library, thank you. Check it out; it's a fantastic library. We also greatly appreciate the use of the beautiful image resources from Photospin.com—check them out as well.

To the team at Peachpit, many thanks for helping us produce this book. It's amazing to think that we are separated by 7940 miles (that's 12,776 km) and yet feel so close via email and FTP. Thanks to Rebecca Gulick for her ongoing patience and guidance, as well as David Van Ness and others at Peachpit.

And a huge thanks to Brie Gyncild, our wordsmith, who translated our projects and Aussie slang from videos into easy-to-follow prose.

And finally let's all do something positive for this wonderful world we live on, earth needs some care and attention, and we all need to get involved.

—*Wayne Rankin*

Many thanks to my fellow authors Wayne and Jack whom I am still shocked and thrilled about being able to work with. It has been a real dream come true in both cases. I would also like to thank them both for helping me stack on an extra 5kg in lard while traveling with them around Australia and New Zealand.

I would also like to send a big thank you to the great folks at Peachpit, Rebecca and the gang for another job well done.

Brie Gyncild has also done another amazing job interpreting such uninterpretable material into some pretty great lessons, tips, and insights. Thank you so much, Brie. You are a top Sheila.

Thanks also to the folks at Adobe Systems, Michael Stoddard and Jane Brady. Also the world-famous Russell Preston Brown for his inspiration and support. Thanks for your support.

I have many great clients here in Australia in many industries including publishers, designers, and advertising agencies, and I would like to thank them!

Without the support of my family immediate and extended, however, the book would not have happened. Thanks first to the most beautiful woman in the world, my smart, fun, sexy and loving wife Nic. Also to my two little angels Abbey and James. I would also like to thank Jim and Judy (my parents) too. Finally a big thanks must go to my brother James in Switzerland, who sent a couple of images he took in the Alps for use in one of our projects. See if you can spot them in Chapter 6.

—*Mike McHugh*

To Wayne, Mike, and Brie, who really put this whole book together.

To Wayne, a close friend, and a world-renowned graphic designer of epic proportions (if not stature), who art directed this book (masochism runs in his family). Mike, as mentioned earlier, is one of Australia's top creative software educators, and the perfect one to shape the projects into accessible step-by-step tutorials. And Brie, who sculpted the actual words that are about to change the way that you think about Adobe Photoshop Elements, is a trooper (as well as an incredible writer) for throwing herself into the middle of all the content coming from three very different crazy creatives.

And me, well, having taught about Elements' big brother, Photoshop, for about a zillion years (now you know how old I am!) and written the *How to Wow: Photoshop for Photography* book (with another phenomenal coauthor, Ben Willmore), as well as the *Adobe Photoshop Elements One-Click Wow!* book, I had plenty of material to contribute to this project. But, information without the blood, sweat, and tears to shape it into the incredibly useful and inspirational work that you hold in your hands doesn't mean a whole lot. I am truly fortunate to be associated with the "Wonda's from Down Unda," along with Brie and all the unshakable pros at Peachpit Press. Thanks for letting me play with you all!

—*Jack Davis*

Contents

6 CREATIVE PRESENTATION 154

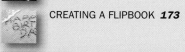

Introduction

DIGITAL PHOTOGRAPHERS, CREATIVE PEOPLE, DESIGNERS, retouchers, digital scrapbookers, and general creative roust-abouts (that includes about 6 billion of us), get excited, because this book and Photoshop Elements 5.0 are going to capture your imagination. You'll find a tremendous variety of projects to choose from. Some are meant for digital photography and some help you retouch and restore old photographs. And in some cases, we start from scratch to create personalized wrapping paper, greeting cards, and other custom masterpieces. Of course, we have provided many tips for everyone about color and workflow issues as well.

The How to Wow manifesto

The How to Wow team works with three goals in mind: quality, flexibility, and speed.

Quality: There are many ways to do similar things in Photoshop Elements. Some of them, however, are just plain wrong. We may not even mention the wrong way to do something, preferring to emphasize the quality approach. If it seems we have skipped over something, it's possible that it's an oversight, but it's more likely we prefer a different way. For example, we prefer to use levels rather than brightness and contrast adjustments.

Flexibility: We here at How to Wow are pixel pacifists. We don't like harming pixels or their environment (Photoshop Elements). Therefore, rest assured that no pixels were harmed in the creation of this book. We always keep a copy of every image in its original high-resolution, layered, and uncompressed state. We use adjustment layers wherever possible, and when it's not possible, we duplicate layers so we always have recourse for change at any stage.

Speed: It always takes longer to cook a meal the first time you follow a recipe. Think of the book as your digital cookbook. After you get the hang of the step-by-step recipes, you will be able to reproduce the methods on your own creations at lightning speed. Not only that—you will begin to throw in your own herbs and spices before too long and become a digital gourmet.

What to Expect

Expect to be surprised. You will create artwork that impresses your harshest critic. With creative people, we're often our own worst critic. If you are self-taught, there is always a lingering doubt, as you wonder whether you are going about things the correct way. We're here to reassure. After working through the chapters in this book, you can expect to be more confident that you are going about things the best way possible.

But Wait... There's More

To complete this book and its lessons successfully, you will need to do at least two things. The first is to start from the start and don't skip anything! We include valuable tips and insights throughout the book, and we'd hate for you to miss anything.

Second, load the contents of the How to Wow CD onto your hard drive. We've provided some great stuff for you to use and explore: styles, textures, custom shapes, and more. We'll use some of these goodies in the projects, but we've included many more to get your creative

juices flowing. Make sure to review the part called Using How to Wow Presets [page 125] in Chapter 4, "Photo Enhancing."

Start Your Own Digital Odyssey

Most of the images in this book have been captured by Jack, Wayne, or Mike on their various travels around this amazing planet. Whether the images celebrated the birth of a grandson or a fabulous holiday or business trip, these photos are similar to those any of us may have taken. You can use the techniques in this book on your own images.

Let your imagination run wild with each new project you try. Before long, you will be master of your own digital domain.

1

PHOTOSHOP ELEMENTS ESSENTIALS

Putting the Mechanics on Autopilot So You Can Get On with Being Creative

RAISE YOUR HAND if you've got a digital camera. Right, just about everyone has one these days. Now, raise your hand if you have figured out how to organize, sort, and manage all of the 1,256,280 images you have clogging up your computer. Ah yes, that's where it gets trickier. With digital cameras, you don't have to worry about wasting film or the cost of developing it, so you're free to be an enthusiastic photographer. And then you're left with all those photos. If that sounds familiar, this chapter should be a big help to you.

In the following pages, we cover everything you need to know to sort your images so that you can get your hands on the one you want, when you want it. Of course, there's much more to Adobe Photoshop Elements than organizing your photos. This first chapter gives you a valuable guided tour through the workspaces of Photoshop Elements 5.0 and the basic workflows that will help you manage and edit images efficiently. We know that becoming familiar with an application as complex as Photoshop Elements is not all beer and skittles, and we're here to make the process easier.

Your New Digital Landscape

Photoshop Elements includes four primary workspaces: the Organizer, Quick Fix, the Photo Editor, and the Creation Wizard. Each is designed to help you perform specific tasks, and each has its own set of tools. We'll show you how each can help you work with your photos.

We'll also use this chapter to show you the basic skills you'll rely on as you work in Photoshop Elements. You'll learn how to make selections, create and manipulate layers, save your images,

and set up color management. Our goal is to help you feel comfortable with the basics so that you're confident and ready to dive in when we introduce cool techniques later in the book.

Viva La Digital Revolution

The digital camera revolution has brought with it a whole new set of file formats and software. Therefore, we need to rethink traditional photography workflows. For example, many digital cameras let you capture the raw data in a proprietary format, giving you much greater flexibility in editing your image. We cover in detail some of the issues and the possibilities that digital photographers and designers face when you work with camera raw formats. We also help you navigate the tools for handling color in a digital environment.

Digital photography is a brave new world. As Jack Davis says, film is just something you find on your teeth. The tips for organizing, managing, and editing your prized digital photos should help you find the prospect of dealing with a thousand images from a single outing less daunting.

Tooling Up

Photoshop Elements includes so many digital gadgets, you may well drool with excitement. Just try not to drool on the keyboard. Take the time to master the information in this first chapter, and you'll be ready to tackle all the projects in the following chapters—and just about any other creative challenge you can think up. The great big world of digital imaging will soon be yours.

The Organizer

Use the Organizer, which includes both the Photo Browser and the Date View workspaces, to sort, search for, tag, and organize your files. Photo Browser displays all the images in a folder or catalog; View By Date displays images in a calendar format.

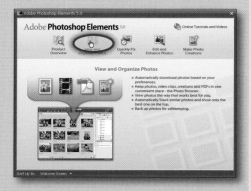

Opening the Organizer

Click View And Organize Photos in the Welcome screen or Photo Browser in the Editor to open the Photo Browser workspace. Click Date View in the Editor to open the Date View workspace.

Importing Images

Click the camera icon **A**, and choose an import method. Most of us import photos directly from a camera or card reader connected to the computer's USB port. But you can also scan traditional photos or copy images from a CD, other portable storage device, or folders on your hard drive. You can import photos from an online sharing service, such as a library of stock photography. You can even download photos from your cell phone, if it includes a camera.

Viewing Images

Photoshop Elements displays thumbnails of your images. Use the scroll bar on the right side of the window to scroll through them **A**. To change the size of the thumbnails, move the slider at the bottom of the screen. To display the smallest thumbnails possible, click the icon to the left of the slider **B**; to display one image at a time, click the icon to the right of the slider **C**.

At the top of the window, the timeline shows when the photographs were taken **D**. The timeline can come in handy for quickly assessing the age of the images. However, if you don't need the timeline, hide it to free up screen real estate by choosing View > Timeline (Ctrl+L).

I N S I G H T

Photos over Time. To view images by date, click the Date View button. Click Day, Month, or Year at the bottom of the window: Day displays images taken on a particular day; scroll through the dates at the top of the window. Month displays thumbnails of the images on the calendar page. Year highlights the dates that photos were taken, but doesn't display thumbnails of those images.

Collections

A collection is a set of images that are related in some way, such as images of a certain place or subject, photos taken at a specific time, or images that you plan to use for a particular project. You can create as many collections as you like, and a photo may be included in multiple collections. To create a collection, choose New > Collections in the Collections palette. To add an image to the collection, select it in the Organizer, and then drag the collection onto it—or drag the image onto the collection. To view the photos in a collection, click the box next to its name in the Collections palette; a binoculars icon appears next to the collection that is currently displayed.

A small number appears on each thumbnail, indicating the order of the images in a collection. To change the order, drag a thumbnail into its new position. The numbers automatically change.

Tagging Images

You can further sort images by applying tags to them. Photoshop Elements includes tags for one-star to five-star ratings, as well as tags for labeling family, friends, places, and events. To create a custom tag, choose New > New Tag in the Tags palette, assign it to a category, and name the tag.

To apply a tag to a photo, drag the tag onto the photo, or drag the photo onto the tag. The star ratings also have keyboard shortcuts; select a photo and press 1 to apply one star, 2 to apply two stars, and so on.

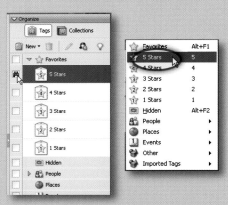

Tagging Faces

Quickly identify and assign tags to photos that include people.

1. Find the Faces.

It's often useful to tag photos with the names of the people who are in them, so that you can easily search for photos later. To find the photos that include people, first display your photos in the Photo Browser. Then, click the Find Faces For Tagging icon in the Tags palette. Photoshop Elements searches the photos in the Organizer for any that contain faces and opens the Face Tagging dialog box A.

2. Create Tags, As Needed.

Each image can have multiple tags assigned to it. You can create a tag for each person in your photos (for example, "Jimmy"), and you can create tags for groups (for example, "great-aunts"). In fact, you can create any tag you want to use, in any category, for the images that contain people. To create a tag, choose New > New Tag in the Tags palette, and then name the tag and assign it to a category B.

When you first create a tag, it's labeled with a question mark.

3. Tag Faces.

Tag faces in the Face Tagging dialog box just as you tag images in the Photo Browser. Simply drag a tag onto an image C. The first image you apply a tag to becomes the icon for that tag D. When you tag a face, Photoshop Elements removes it from the Face Tagging dialog box so that you can clearly see which faces remain untagged.

When you select a face, a thumbnail of the full photo appears in the lower-right corner of the dialog box. Click that thumbnail to select all the faces that appear in that photo.

T I P

See More Faces. By default, Photoshop Elements finds faces that are relatively large in a photograph. If you want to find more faces, including smaller faces in the background of images, press Ctrl as you click Find Faces For Tagging. Photoshop Elements will provide more accurate results, but it will take longer to display all the faces.

T I P

See Tagged Faces. If you want to see the faces you've tagged, select Show Already Tagged Faces at the top of the Face Tagging dialog box. Photoshop Elements sorts the faces according to the tag you've assigned. Untagged images are displayed at the top.

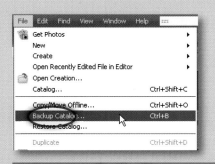

Stacking Related Images

If you take multiple photos that are similar—for example, several photos of a child in the same pose—you may want to stack those images together so that they are easier to manage. Stacking images lets you find the entire set easily, without cluttering up the Photo Browser.

To create a stack, select the photos you want to include (press Ctrl to select multiple images), right-click the photo you want to display in the Photo Browser, and then choose Stack > Stack Selected Photos (or Ctrl+Alt+S). A rhombus icon appears in the corner of the thumbnail of the top photo in the stack. To unstack photos, right-click the stack and choose Stack > Unstack Photos.

Backing Up Photos

Your digital photos are as vulnerable as any other electronic data, and often far more precious. You don't want to lose those memories when a hard drive fails or your laptop is stolen. So back up those images to CD, portable hard drives, or other devices. In the Organizer, choose File > Backup. You can back up your entire catalog onto a CD, DVD, or separate hard disk. If you have too much information to fit onto a DVD, invest in a removable hard drive. Later, if you lose your originals, choose File > Restore in the Organizer to recover them from your backup.

T I P

Share the Memories. Share your photos with family, friends, or colleagues on a CD or DVD. In the Organizer, select the files you want to share, choose File > Burn, select Copy/Move Files, and then click Next. Don't select anything on the next screen unless you want to move, rather than copy, your files. We recommend leaving the files on your hard drive in most cases, so click Next again. Then, insert the blank disc, name the set of photos, and click Done to burn the disc.

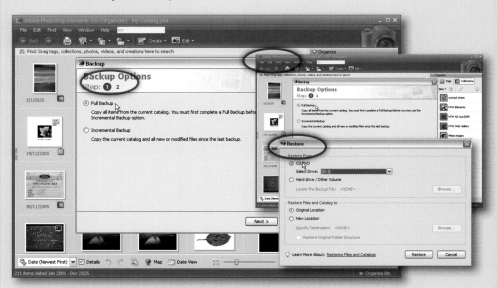

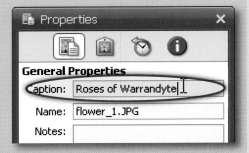

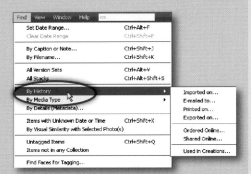

Adding Captions to Images

Captions help viewers understand when or where a picture was taken, who's in it, or what's going on. They also make it easier to search for a particular image later. To add a caption to an image, right-click it, choose Add Caption, and type the caption—up to 2000 characters. Or, type the caption directly on screen when you're viewing a single image in the Organizer. Use the Properties palette if you want to type a caption and add other information about the image: choose Window > Properties to open the palette.

Searching for Images

Search for a particular image by keywords, its captions, the date it was taken, or metadata. Choose Find > By Filename if you know the name of the image file. Choose Find > By History to search for images imported or emailed on a specific date. Choose Find > By Media Type to look for files of a specific type, such as PDF files. Choose Find > By Detail to search by camera make, author, or any other metadata field. You can even search for photos that are visually similar to a photo you've selected. 🖦

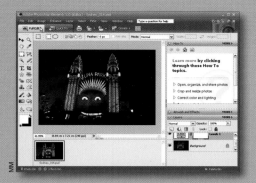

The Editor

Use the Editor, which includes the Standard Edit and Quick Fix workspaces, to enhance photos, create special effects, correct color problems, and perform other editing tasks.

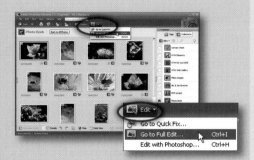

Opening the Editor

To open the Editor, select one or more images in the Organizer and click Edit > Go to Quick Fix or Edit > Go to Standard Edit. The images you selected open in the Standard Edit workspace.

From the Standard Edit workspace, you can go to the Photo Browser or Date View workspaces in the Organizer. Images that are currently open in the Editor appear with a padlock icon in the Organizer to show that they are being edited and cannot be moved or changed in the Organizer.

Viewing Images

Select the image you want to work with from the Photo Bin at the bottom of the window. You can scroll through the open images without viewing each one.

To view multiple windows simultaneously, click the Tile or Cascade icon in the upper-right corner. Press the spacebar to pan within an individual image window; press the spacebar and the Shift key to pan all the image windows at the same time.

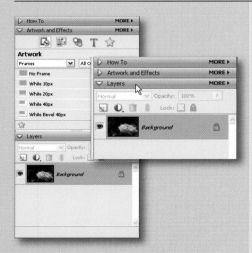

Working with Palettes

The Palette Bin, on the right side of the window, contains the palettes you use to edit images. You can dock palettes in the bin and collapse them using the arrows. Or, if you prefer to use floating palettes, drag a palette out onto the screen; then you can resize and reposition it. To dock a palette again, drag it on top of the bin.

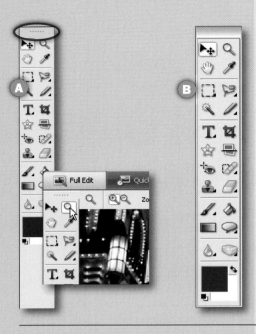

The Toolbox

You'll find your editing tools in the toolbox on the left side of the screen. By default, it's a double column of tools docked at the left of screen **A**. To transform it into a two-column, floating toolbox **B**, click the dotted line at the top of the toolbox and drag it onto the screen. To return it to its original position, drag it to the left side and it will pop into place.

Hover over a tool to see its keyboard shortcut. As you select a tool, the Options bar at the top of the screen displays the options for that tool. For example, when the Crop tool is selected, you can change the aspect ratio and width and height in the Options bar.

Quick Fix Workspace

The Quick Fix workspace gives you the tools to quickly remedy common photo problems. As in the Standard Edit workspace, there is a Photo Bin to let you move from one open image to another. However, the toolbox is much smaller, there are fewer brushes available, and instead of the Palette Bin, settings for specific adjustments are on the right side of the window.

The Quick Fix workspace includes handy viewing options so that you can see exactly how you're affecting your original image. We recommend choosing the Before And After (Landscape) or Before And After (Portrait) option from the View menu, depending on the orientation of your image.

Organizing Your Workflow

Wrangle those digital photos into order using the Organizer. Taking a few minutes to tag them now will make it easier to find them later.

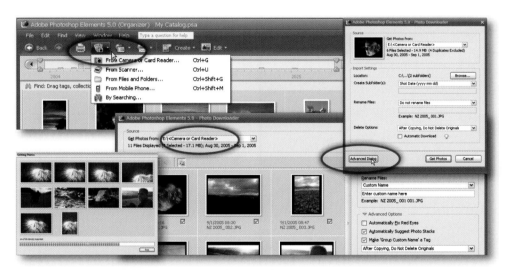

1. Import Images into the Organizer.

Open the Organizer by clicking View and Organize Photos in the Welcome screen or Organize in the Editor workspace. Click the camera icon and choose From Camera or Card Reader. Then, in the Photo Downloader dialog box, select your camera or card reader. Create a subfolder for the images and name it. Click Advanced Dialog for more options, including automatic red eye fix. (We prefer to fix red eye ourselves, and we'll show you how to do it later in the book!) Then, click Get Photos. Delete any images that you don't want to import from the list that appears. You can also delete them from the camera or card reader, but we prefer to make sure our images have downloaded properly before deleting them from the original source.

When you've imported the images, they appear in the Organizer. Only the images you've just imported appear. Click Back To All Photos whenever you want to work with your entire image catalog.

T I P

Apply Metadata on Import. Claim your glory and protect your copyright without having to type the information for each photograph. When you import images from a camera or card scanner, click Advanced Dialog to display more options. Then, enter the photographer's name and copyright information. Photoshop Elements applies the data to each of the images you import, and the metadata travels with the image.

2. Create a Collection.

Click the Collections button in the Organize Bin, and then choose New > New Collection, and name the collection. At first, the icon is a question mark because there's no content in the collection. To add an image to the collection—and create the icon for it—drag the question mark onto an image; a thumbnail of that image becomes the icon for the collection. To add other images, select them and drag the icon onto them. To add all the images in the window to the collection, press Ctrl+A to select them all, and then drag the icon onto one of them.

To display the collection, click the box next to it in the Collections palette; a binoculars icon appears.

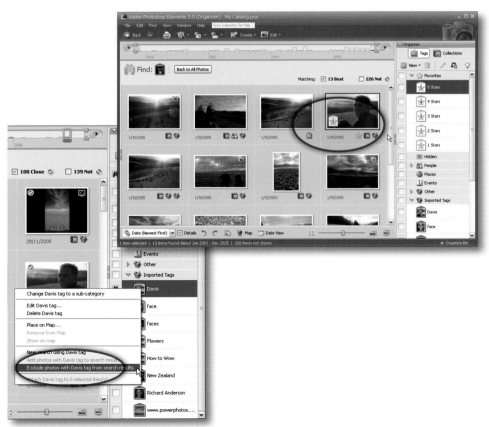

3. Tag Images.

Apply tags to images to identify and sort them. Photoshop Elements includes tags for one-star to five-star ratings, as well as tags for labeling family, friends, places, and events. You can also import tags that are already attached to images, or import an entire set of tags. Click the Tags button in the Organize Bin. To apply a tag to a photo, drag the tag icon onto the photo, or drag the photo onto the icon. To create a custom tag, choose New > New Tag, assign it to a category, and name the tag. When you apply a tag to the first image, a thumbnail of that image becomes the tag's icon.

To see the images associated with a tag, click the box next to that tag in the Tags palette. To narrow your search further, select another tag. Photoshop Elements displays only those images that are associated with both tags. To exclude photos with a certain tag, right-click the tag in the Tags palette and choose Exclude Photos With [tag] From Search Results.

4. Evaluate Your Photos.

To determine which images require editing, click the icon to the right of the thumbnail slider to see a single image a time. Scroll through the images, typing a caption for each one. When you see one that needs some adjustment, choose Edit > Go To Quick Fix. The image opens in the Quick Fix workspace. Make a quick adjustment to the image, such as applying Smart Fix, and then choose File > Save. Photoshop Elements saves the new version in the same folder as the original; select Save In Version Set With Original to be able to compare the versions easily later. Choose Photoshop (PSD) format, and then click Save.

The new version appears in the Organizer, with a Version Set icon in the upper-right corner. Right-click the image and choose Version Set > Reveal Items in Version Set to see the before and after versions of the file. ▥

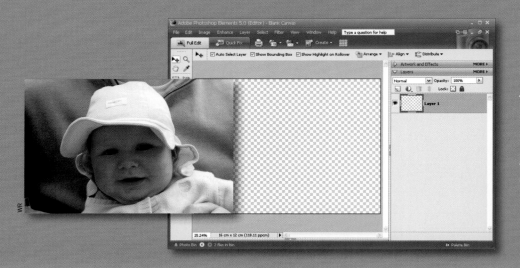

Creating a New Document

Begin with a blank canvas, onto which you can copy and paste images, add layers, and create text.

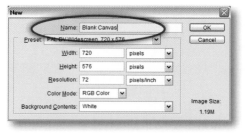

1. Create the Document.

Choose File > New > Blank File, or press Ctrl+N. Photoshop Elements opens the Editor and displays the New dialog box. Name the file.

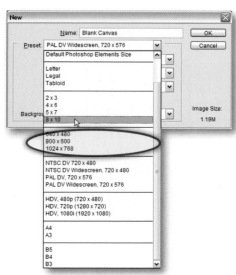

2. Select a Canvas Size.

Select a size for your blank canvas from the Preset menu, or type values for the height and width. Preset values include standard photo frame sizes, such as 8 x 10 inches; standard paper sizes, such as Letter or A4; standard computer screen sizes, such as 800 x 600; and standard video sizes, such as NTSC DV Widescreen 720 x 480. Choose one of these or type your own height and width values in inches, centimeters, pixels, picas, or another unit.

3. Type a Resolution.

Type a resolution in the Resolution text box. The default resolution is 72 pixels per inch **A**, which is an appropriate resolution for images that will be viewed only on screen. However, if you plan to print your image, especially if you're going to send the image to a professional printer, set a resolution of 300 pixels per inch **B**. For printing to a desktop printer, you may achieve good quality with a resolution of 225 pixels per inch **C**, but we recommend 300 pixels per inch.

The resolution affects the image size, which is shown in the lower-right corner of the dialog box. Larger images take longer to open and, in general, slow the performance of your computer.

4. Choose a Color Mode.

The color mode determines the range of colors available for the image. Choose Bitmap if you want only to work with black and white **A**; choose Grayscale for black-and-white images that include grays **B**. Choose RGB Color for any image that will include colors other than black, white, and gray **C**.

It's harder to add color than to remove it, so if you're not sure whether your final image will be grayscale or color, we recommend choosing RGB Color.

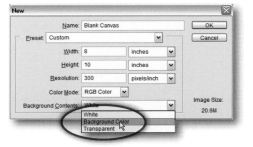

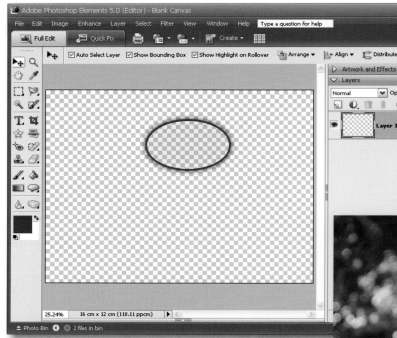

5. Choose the Background.

Your blank canvas isn't actually empty; it has a background. Choose Transparent to make the background invisible; choose White to start with a white background; or choose Background Color to apply the background color shown in the toolbox. If you choose Transparent, Photoshop Elements displays the background with the checkerboard pattern that indicates transparency.

Click OK to open the new canvas.

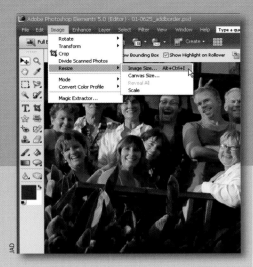

Resizing an Image

The image size of an image is a measure of the number of pixels along its width and height. How you resize an image determines its resolution and print quality.

Viewing the Image Size

You can see how many pixels are in an image, the document size, and the image resolution in the Image Size dialog box. Choose Image > Resize > Image Size (or press Ctrl+Alt+I).

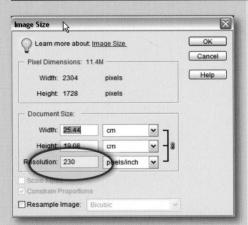

Increasing the Image Resolution

When you resize an image, consider the effect on the resolution. For example, many images are 230 pixels per inch, a resolution that's standard for digital prints but not high enough for use on a printing press. You can reduce the document's width and height, and increase the resolution: Deselect Resample Image, and then type 300 for the resolution. Photoshop Elements automatically changes the width and height in proportion with the new resolution.

Resampling an image either throws away detail to lower the resolution or adds detail to increase the resolution. Either way, the image loses some of its integrity.

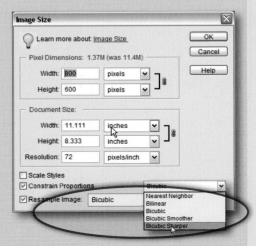

Decreasing the Image Resolution

If you're working with an image that will only be viewed on screen, you may want to downsample the image to 72 pixels per inch. Select Resample Image in the Image Size dialog box, and then type 72 ppi for the resolution. The width and height remain the same, though the resolution has changed.

We recommend using the Bicubic Sharper option if you must downsample an image, as this method of downsampling keeps the image sharp. If you must upsample an image, use Bicubic Smoother.

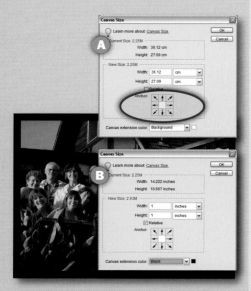

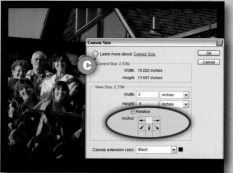

Resizing the Canvas

Changing the canvas size doesn't affect the size of the image itself, but you can reduce the canvas size to crop part of your image, or increase it to add a border or increase the background. To change the canvas size, choose Image > Resize > Canvas Size.

In the Canvas Size dialog box, you'll see the current canvas dimensions, which are originally the same as the image dimensions **A**. For Anchor, click the square where you want to position the image on the new canvas. For example, if you want to add an even border around the image **B**, click the center square to center the image. Then click Relative and type 1" for both the width and the height. Photoshop Elements adds half an inch to the canvas in every direction, and it's colored the same as the background color. We can choose black, instead, to give our image a nice black border. To add space for a caption at the bottom **C**, select the top square in the Anchor, and change the height to add the needed space.

> ### INSIGHT
>
> **Resize in the Image Size Dialog Box.** The Image Size dialog box gives you greater control over resampling options than the Save For Web feature. Even if you plan to use that feature later, we recommend using the Image Size dialog box to resize your image.

Scaling an Image

To scale an image, choose Image > Resize > Scale. Hold down the Shift key and drag the edge of the image or type new values in the Options bar, and then click the check mark to confirm the transformation. You can scale all layers except the background layer; if the photo contains only one layer, Photoshop Elements will ask whether you want to make the background a layer, and if you click OK, it unlocks and renames the layer. ▥

Making a Selection

To edit an area of an image, you must first select it. There are several selection tools and methods in Photoshop Elements.

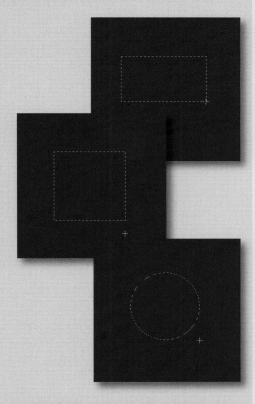

Marquee Tools

Use the Rectangular and Elliptical Marquee tools to create square, circular, rectangular, or elliptical selections. These tools work well for cropping images, in particular, and provide a quick way to select an area for editing.

Select a Marquee tool and drag it on the screen. To create a perfect square or circle, hold down the Shift key as you drag the tool. To draw from the center outward, hold down the Alt key as you drag the tool. And, of course, to draw a perfect square or circle from the center outward, hold down both the Shift and Alt keys as you drag.

Lasso Tool	L
Magnetic Lasso Tool	L
Polygonal Lasso Tool	L

T I P

Moving a Selection. Sometimes a selection isn't quite in the right place, especially when you're selecting a tricky object, such as an eye. To reposition a selection, press the spacebar and then drag the selection.

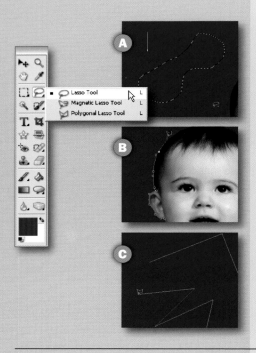

Lasso Tools

The Lasso A, Magnetic Lasso B, and Polygonal Lasso C tools draw irregular selections.

With the Lasso tool, you can draw a freehand shape.

The Magnetic Lasso tool snaps to the edge between contrasting colors. To use the tool, click it next to the area you want to select. For example, if you want to draw a selection around a person, click next to the person. Then, drag the tool around the edge of the object, clicking occasionally so that you can backtrack easily if you need to. This tool works best when there is a clear contrast between the area you're selecting and its background.

The Polygonal Lasso tool draws straight lines between points where you click. Click an initial point, and then click each time you want to create a straight edge for your selection. Click on the starting point again, or double-click anywhere, to complete the selection.

> **TIP**
>
> **Clearing a Selection.** To remove a selection and start over again, choose Select > Deselect, or press Ctrl+D.

Selection Brushes

The Selection Brush and Magic Selection Brush tools are different from other selection tools. Rather than drag a selection around a shape, you paint over that shape. The area you paint over becomes the selection.

To use the Selection Brush, set the brush size and type in the Options bar A, and then paint over the area you want to select. The selection appears as you paint.

To use the Magic Selection Brush, set the brush size and type in the Options bar, and then paint or scribble over the area you want to select B. Colored strokes appear where you paint; when you release the mouse, Photoshop Elements analyzes the area you painted and selects the area that matches its color and texture. You may need to experiment with this tool a little bit to get the hang of it, but because you needn't paint precisely, this tool can save you time.

> **INSIGHT**
>
> **Feathering a Selection.** Sometimes you may want to feather your selection, so that effects you apply to it fade gradually at the edges. If you're using a Marquee or Lasso tool to make the selection, simply type a value for Feather in the Options bar. If you're using the Selection Brush tool, decrease the Hardness value of the brush in the Options bar.

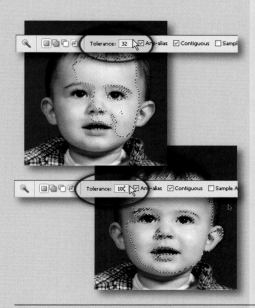

Magic Wand

Use the Magic Wand tool to select a large area quickly. This tool is commonly used to remove a background, for example. Click somewhere in the area you want to select; the Magic Wand tool selects everything that is similar in color and texture to the area you clicked. If too much or too little is selected, adjust the Tolerance value, which determines how similar pixels must be to be included. With a tolerance level of 100, the selection includes greater variation than it does at 50.

In the Options bar, select Anti-Alias if you want the edges of the selection to be smoothed. Select Contiguous to select only pixels that are next to each other, without interruption. Select Sample All Layers if you want to select the same area on all layers of your image.

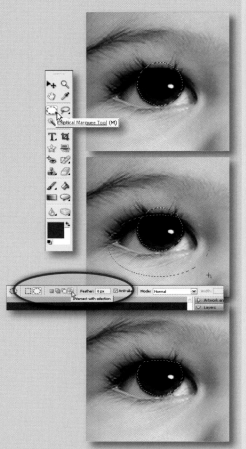

Add, Subtract, and Intersect

You can fine-tune a selection by adding to it or subtracting from it. For example, to select an eye, you might create a perfect circle selection and then subtract an oval from the selection where the eyelid appears.

When a selection tool is selected in the toolbox, the Add, Subtract, and Intersect options are available in the Options bar.

To add to a selection, click Add To Selection in the Options bar, and make another selection. Or, hold down the Shift key, and then select the area and make another selection.

To subtract from a selection, click Subtract From Selection in the Options bar, and make another selection. Or, hold down the Alt key, and then select the area and make another selection.

To create a selection from the area where two selections overlap, click Intersect With Selection in the Options bar, and make the second selection. Or, hold down the Alt and Shift keys, and then select the area and make the second selection. ▥

Replacing a Background

Use the Magic Wand tool to remove the background from an image, and then place your subject over a different background.

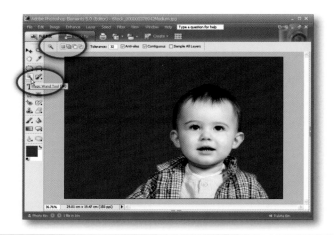

1. Adjust the Settings for the Magic Wand Tool.

Open the *01-boy.psd* file from the *How to Wow Photoshop Elements* DVD. Select the Magic Wand tool. In the Options bar, adjust the tolerance for the background you're selecting. If it's a single color, use a lower tolerance. If it's more complex, increase the tolerance. The Magic Wand tool works best when the background is simple, as it is in the image of the young boy.

2. Delete the Background.

The background layer in an image is locked, so to edit it, we must first unlock it. Double-click the background layer in the Layers palette, and then rename it "Boy." The padlock symbol no longer appears next to the layer. Now, click the Magic Wand tool in the background area. It selects the entire background. Press the Delete key, and the background is replaced with the checkerboard pattern that indicates transparency.

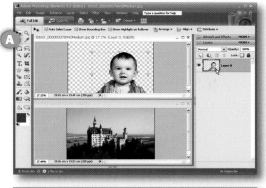

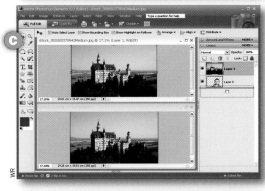

3. Add the New Background.

Let's make our young boy a world traveler. Open the *01-castle.psd* file. Choose Window > Images > Tile to see both images **A**. Drag the castle layer from the Layers palette onto the image of the boy in the image window **B**. Photoshop Elements automatically adds the castle layer above the layer we called Boy, so the boy disappears behind the castle **C**. Move the new layer beneath the Boy layer in the Layers palette, so that the boy appears on top **D**. Now, select the Move tool, select Auto Select Layer in the Options bar, and move the Boy layer where you want it to appear in front of the castle. ▦

Working with Layers

Layers are powerful because they let you make changes to your image without altering the original, so you can experiment with confidence.

Creating Layers

When you first open an image, it has a single background layer. To add a layer, click the Create A New Layer icon at the top of the palette, and then type a name for it. If you want to be prompted for a name when you create a layer, press the Alt key as you click the Create A New Layer icon.

You can add a layer from another image. Open both images in Photoshop Elements, and tile them on the screen **A**. Then, drag a layer from one image onto the other image in the Image window **B**. Photoshop Elements automatically adds the new layer to the image.

T I P

Float the Palette. By default, the Layers palette is docked in the Palette Bin on the right side of the window, but you can move it anywhere you want. When you drag the palette out of the bin, it becomes a floating palette that you can resize and reposition wherever it's handiest for you. To dock the Layers palette again, just drag its tab over the bin; it will pop back into place.

Layer Options

Use the Layers palette to change the appearance of the layer.

To show or hide a layer, click the box next to it in the Layers palette. An eye icon appears next to layers that are visible.

To rename a layer, double-click its name and type a new name.

To delete a layer, select it and then click the Delete Layer icon at the top of the palette.

To change the opacity of a layer, select the layer in the Layers palette and then either move the Opacity slider or type a percentage. The lower the opacity, the more transparent the layer.

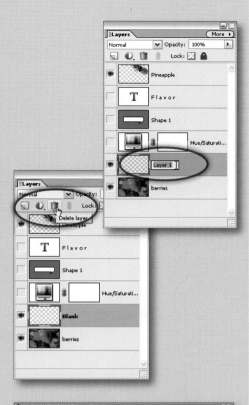

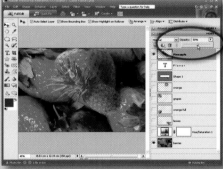

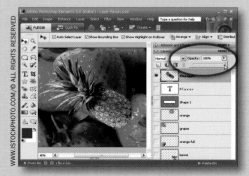

Manipulating Layers

You can move, scale, link, group, and rearrange layers.

To move a layer, select the Move tool and make sure Auto Select Layer is selected in the Options bar. Then, click an object in the Image window **A**. When you click the object, its entire layer is automatically selected, so as you move it, the entire layer shifts.

To scale a layer, first display the layer's bounding box: select the Move tool, and then select Show Bounding Box in the Options bar. With the Move tool, click an object on the layer **B**. Then, drag the layer's bounding box to resize it. To scale it proportionally, press the Shift key as you drag.

To link layers, press the Shift key as you select them, and then right-click and choose Link Layers **C**. You can move linked layers together in the Layers palette and in the Image window. To unlink layers, right-click a linked layer and choose Unlink Layers.

To unlock a background layer so that you can make it transparent, double-click the layer and give it a new name.

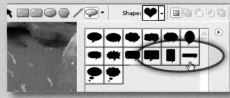

Vector Shape Layers

A vector shape layer is not made up of pixels. Instead, it's composed of points and handles, so that you can resize it without worrying about resolution. When you draw a shape with the Rectangle, Rounded Rectangle, Ellipse, Polygon, Line, or Custom Shape tool, Photoshop Elements automatically places that shape on a new vector shape layer.

The shape takes the foreground color shown in the Toolbox A. To change the color, double-click the object and then sample a color from the color picker B, or from an object in your image.

The Custom Shape tool includes several shapes, including butterflies and speech bubbles. Select the shape you want to use from the Options bar.

Adjustment Layers

An adjustment layer is a layer that contains settings, but no objects. You can use an adjustment layer to apply settings to the layers beneath it without affecting those layers.

To create an adjustment layer, click the Create Adjustment Layer icon in the Layers palette, and then choose a type of adjustment layer. Photoshop Elements creates a new layer and opens a dialog box where you select your settings. For example, if you create a Hue/Saturation adjustment layer, Photoshop Elements opens the Hue/Saturation dialog box.

By default, an adjustment layer affects all the layers beneath it in the Layers palette. However, you can group it with a particular layer if you want it to affect only that one layer. To group layers, hold down the Alt key and click between the layers. A small arrow appears on the layer in the Layers palette to indicate that it is grouped with the layer below it.

Text Layers

To create text, select the Horizontal or Vertical Type tool, and then click an insertion point or draw a text box on the screen. Photoshop Elements automatically creates a new layer for your text and names it with the text you type.

You can choose font, type size, and other type characteristics from the Options bar. ▣

Saving an Image

Save an image so that you can return to it to make additional edits later.

1. Choose File > Save As.

When you've made changes to your document that you want to keep, choose File > Save As. In the Save As dialog box, select a folder to save to, and name the document. If you want to be able to work with the file in the Photoshop Elements Organizer, select Include In The Organizer.

2. Save the File in a Version Set.

If you're making multiple changes, you can save each version with the original so that you can easily make comparisons later. Select Save In Version Set With Original.

To view photos in a version set, right-click a version set in the Photo Browser, and choose Version Set > Reveal Items In Version Set.

3. Choose a Format.

Choose a format and click Save. We recommend saving in Photoshop (.PSD) format if you may want to edit the image again later. Even if you are preparing a final JPEG file for use on a Web site, for example, save the final version as a PSD file first, so that you can return to it in the future. A Photoshop file includes all the layers, and you can include the ICC profile for color management.

If you need to compress the file, save as a JPEG or JPEG 2000 file. However, both of these formats result in some data loss every time you save in this format, so use this format only for a final version of the file. Layers are flattened when you save a JPEG file.

Photoshop PDF is a great option if you need to share your artwork with someone who doesn't have Photoshop or Photoshop Elements. A Photoshop PDF file can be viewed in the free Adobe Reader, but it retains layers and includes the ICC profile.

If you're going to place your image in Adobe PageMaker or QuarkXPress, you may need to save the file as a Photoshop EPS file. If you're working with Adobe InDesign, you can place a Photoshop PSD file. 🏁

T I P

Save a Copy. You can save a copy of your file, while leaving the original open. Select As A Copy in the Save As dialog box to save a copy of the file to the folder that contains the file that is currently open.

Managing Colors

If you want your printed photos to match what you see on the screen, you'll want to use color management. Color management maps the colors that your camera recognizes with the colors that your monitor can use, and then maps those colors to the ones that are available to your printer.

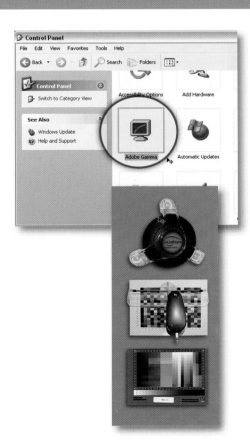

T I P

Check the Profile. Many images have profiles embedded from the camera that took them, or from editing in Photoshop or Photoshop Elements. To see which profile is embedded in an image, choose Document Profile from the pop-up menu at the bottom of the image.

---

1. Create Device Profiles.

Key to color management are the device profiles that describe the colors that are available to your camera, scanner, monitor, and printer. You can use the profiles that the manufacturer provides, but it's best to create one for your particular device, as they may change over time.

You can use hardware to calibrate your monitor and create the most accurate device profiles, but those are expensive. If you don't have the hardware tools, use Adobe Gamma in Windows to generate a monitor profile. Adobe Gamma is automatically installed in the Windows Control Panel when you install Photoshop Elements. To open it, choose Start > Settings > Control Panel, and then double-click Adobe Gamma. Then click Step by Step (Wizard) and follow the on-screen instructions to create a custom profile.

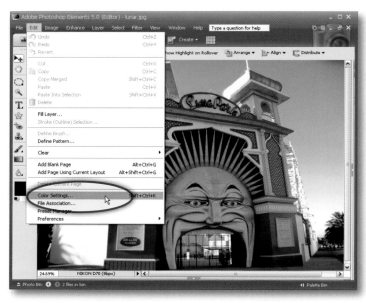

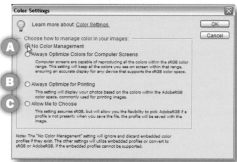

2. Choose Color Settings.

In Photoshop Elements, choose Edit > Color Settings. These settings determine how Photoshop Elements manages color. Select Always Optimize For Printing **B**, if you plan to print your images; Photoshop Elements will display everything in Adobe RGB.

Select Always Optimize Colors For Computer Screens only **A**, if you edit photos that will be viewed only on screens; Photoshop Elements will display everything in the sRGB color space, which has a limited range of colors that is appropriate for display on most computer screens.

Select Allow Me To Choose **C**, if you want to switch back and forth between sRGB and Adobe RGB. To switch, choose Image > Convert Color Profile, and then choose either sRGB or Adobe RGB. Be careful when you convert profiles because you can lose the original color. We recommend sticking with the original color profile and displaying in Adobe RGB.

3. Embed the Profile.

When you save the document, select ICC Profile in the Save As dialog box. The profile is embedded with the document, so it's available when you open the document in Photoshop Elements, print it, or place it into an application that supports color management, such as Adobe InDesign. ▥

Working with Camera Raw Files

If your digital camera can save files in a raw format, you have an additional set of tools to finesse the color in your images.

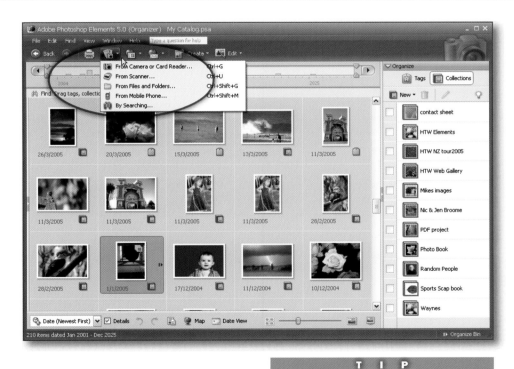

1. Save in Raw Format.

A camera raw file contains picture data exactly as a camera's image sensor captures it, without any processing. Many digital cameras can save raw format files. To see which raw file formats Photoshop Elements supports, visit the Adobe Web site.

Follow the instructions in your camera's manual to set the camera to save files in its own raw file format. Raw files will have file extensions such as NEF or CRW when you download them to your computer.

Choose Import > From Camera Or Card Reader to import the files into the Organizer in Photoshop Elements.

T I P

Rotate Images. To rotate an image, click one of the Rotate Image icons at the top of the window. The left button rotates the image 90 degrees counterclockwise, and the right button rotates it 90 degrees clockwise.

2. Select the Images.

In the Organizer, select the raw images you want to work with. To select multiple images, press the Shift key. Then, click Go To Standard Edit. Photoshop Elements opens images in a raw format in the Camera Raw workspace.

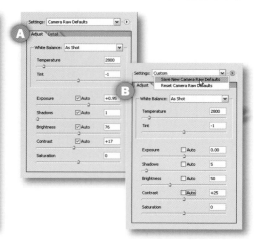

> **INSIGHT**
>
> **Change the Defaults.** When you first open the Camera Raw workspace, all the Auto options are selected **A**. We prefer to see the image in its original state, without any adjustments, when we first open it. To change the default settings, deselect the Auto options or make any other changes you want to set as the defaults, and then choose Save New Camera Raw Defaults **B**, from the Settings menu. If you ever want to return to the original defaults, choose Reset Camera Raw Defaults.

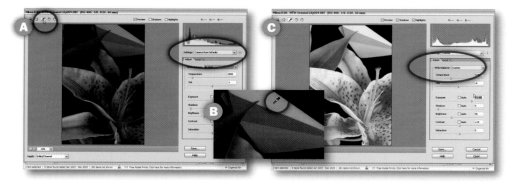

3. Set the White Balance.

The white balance determines the color temperature of the image. The camera records the white balance at the time of exposure **A**, but you can adjust it using the White Balance tool **B**, or the controls on the Adjust tab. To use the White Balance tool, click a neutral area in the image. That area is neutralized and the color temperature of the entire image is adjusted accordingly. Lighter neutrals, such as white areas, work best.

The White Balance tool automatically adjusts the Temperature and Tint settings **C**, but you can tweak them if necessary.

> **INSIGHT**
>
> **White Balance Cards.** If the proper color temperature is important to you, include a neutral card, such as a Whi-Bal card, in one of the photos. Then, click the Whi-Bal card in Photoshop Elements to adjust the white balance.

4. Set the Exposure and Shadow Values.

Move the Exposure slider to change how bright or dark the image is. Move the Shadow slider to change which areas of the image are mapped to black. Essentially, the Exposure slider sets the white point and the Shadow slider sets the black point.

As you move either the Exposure or Shadow slider, you can lose detail in bright areas or shadows. To see where detail is lost, select both Shadows and Highlights at the top of the window. When these options are selected, Photoshop Elements highlights bright areas that are missing detail in red and dark areas that are missing detail in blue. Because our eyes expect to see more detail in bright areas than in shadows, it's more important that the detail remain intact in bright areas.

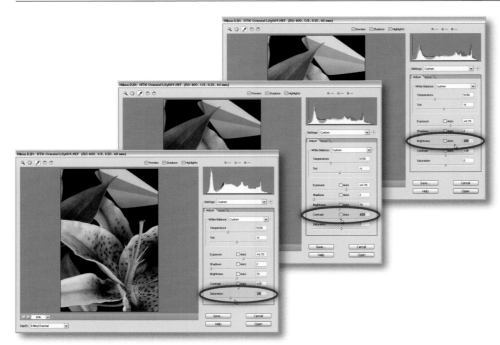

5. Set the Brightness, Contrast, and Saturation Values.

Move the Brightness, Contrast, and Saturation sliders to fine-tune the tones in your image.

The Brightness slider brightens the image as a whole by compressing the highlights and expanding the shadows.

The Contrast slider changes the contrast in the midtones, which are the tones between the highlights and the shadows.

The Saturation slider adjusts the color saturation of the image. If you move the slider to the far left, the image appears to be grayscale; if you move it to the far right, the color saturation is doubled.

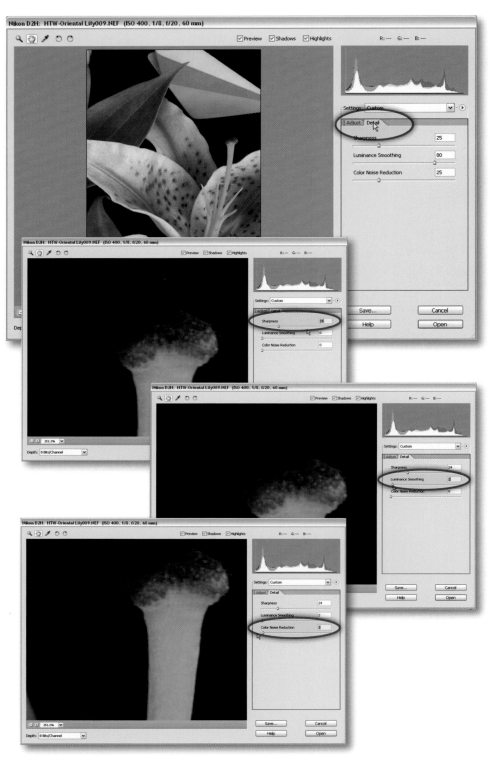

6. Set Options on the Detail Tab.

Click the Detail tab, and adjust the sharpness, luminance smoothing, and color noise reduction.

Many people prefer to sharpen an image after they've made all their changes, but you can also perform some sharpening before making changes in the Photoshop Elements Editor. We recommend sharpening the image less than the default value of 25.

Luminance Smoothing smoothes the detail in the image. A small amount of smoothing, such as a setting of 1, 2, or 3, usually provides the best detail.

Color Noise Reduction minimizes the stray bits of color you may see in dark areas. For most images, you'll have good results with a low setting, such as 1, 2, or 3.

7. Open the Image in the Editor.

When you've made the adjustments in the Camera Raw workspace, click Open to open the adjusted image in the Photoshop Elements Editor. Don't forget to save the image, too, so that you don't lose the changes you've made! 🎞

T I P

Picture the Past. By default, Preview is selected in the Camera Raw workspace, so that you can see the changes you've made. To see the original image, without the adjustments you've made to the raw file, deselect Preview. Then select Preview again to see the current version of the file.

2

PHOTO OPTIMIZING

Add Life to Your Digital Photos. Surprise Everyone!

SEPARATING SCANNED IMAGES *48*

CROPPING WITH CUSTOM SHAPES *50*

CROPPING AND STRAIGHTENING *52*

CORRECTING DISTORTION *55*

FIXING IMAGES QUICKLY *59*

UNDERSTANDING LEVELS *62*

ADJUSTING LIGHTING IN PHOTOS *63*

REMOVING COLOR CASTS *65*

REDUCING NOISE *68*

COLOR CURVES *70*

ABOUT SHARPENING *72*

ADJUSTING HUE AND SATURATION *74*

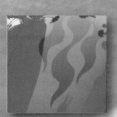

ADDING AN OBJECT TO A PHOTO *77*

WE'RE SURE YOU'LL AGREE that Chapter 2 is always the best, most useful, and most interesting chapter in the book. This Chapter 2 is no exception. We're sure that the tips and techniques it holds are the ones you'll use most frequently on your images.

What, No Tripod?

We don't all have a money tree in the back yard, and though Mike is lucky enough to have one, his wife keeps telling him that the leaves are dropping off. That's why it's great that you don't need a tripod or fancy equipment to get good photos when you have Photoshop Elements. We show you how to quickly fix crooked photos. And if you're converting physical photographs to digital images, you'll learn how to scan several images at a time and then automatically crop and straighten them. We'll also show you how to crop an image into a particular shape, using the Cookie Cutter tool. In fact, we'll introduce you to several ways to crop and rotate images, so that you can get the result you want no matter what the framing problem may be.

Light Saver

Luke, use the levels! When people are new to photography, they tend to underestimate the importance of great lighting. Poor lighting conditions can affect your images in many ways. However, you're not stuck with those bad lighting decisions. You can darken highlights, lighten shadows, and reveal the detail in either. In fact, you can quickly correct most lighting problems by using the shadow and highlight features, understanding the histogram, or taking advantage of the tools in the Quick Fix workspace.

Mike's Favorite Color

Mike's favorite color is neutral gray. What's yours? Blue is a great color, and so are red and yellow. But if you're

removing unwanted color casts from your images, neutral gray can be your best friend. Using various methods, we show you how to quickly and accurately remove these obtrusive spectral phenomena. You can use some of the same methods to retouch and enhance images, as well, but we'll get to that later.

Special Tricks

When you edit photographs digitally, you can create your own reality. In fact, you can add objects that weren't in the original. You can also enhance the intensity of a sky or a crop of lavender, change the color of someone's shirt, or change the perspective of a photo.

We recommend that you learn this chapter well. The techniques it covers are useful on their own, and they'll build the foundation for many of the skills you'll rely on later.

Separating Scanned Images

Quickly straighten and separate multiple scanned images on a page.

1. Place the Photos on the Scanner.

It's almost inevitable that photographs shift on the scanner bed as you lower the lid. Rather than contorting yourself to hold them in place, relax and rely on Photoshop Elements. Clean the glass on your scanner to ensure the images will scan well, and then place as many photos on the scanner bed as will fit.

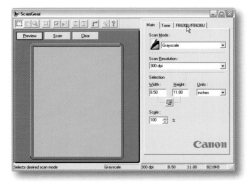

2. Import the Images.

Choose Import > From Scanner to import the images into Photoshop Elements. You'll need to select your scanner and specify settings such as black & white, color, and resolution. For most purposes, we recommend scanning at a resolution of 300 or higher.

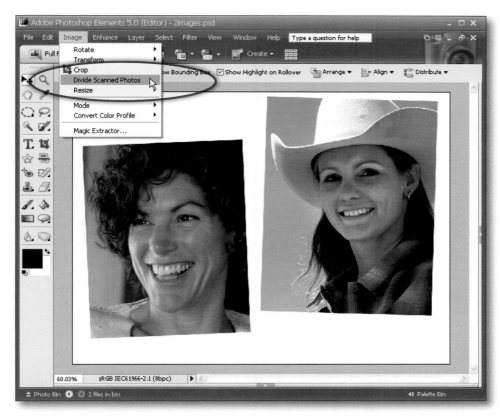

3. Divide the Images.

Choose Image > Divide Scanned Photos. Almost magically, Photoshop Elements identifies the edges of each photo, crops it, copies and pastes it onto a new canvas, and aligns it according to its edges. Each image is now its own file, perfectly aligned, without the skew that may have come from the scanner. (As Photoshop Elements works, you may briefly see the checkerboard pattern that indicates transparency.)

Cropping with Custom Shapes

Use the Cookie Cutter tool to give your photos interesting borders.

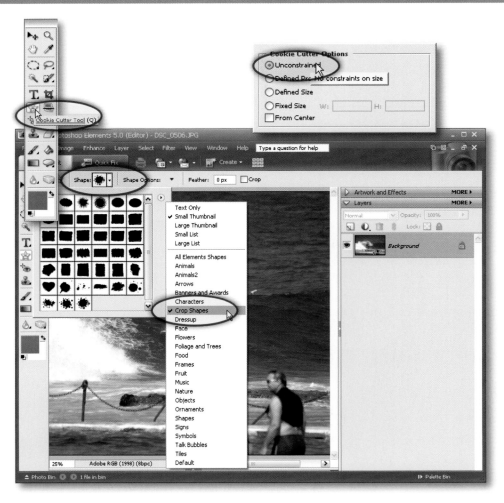

1. Set up the Cookie Cutter Tool.

In the Editor, select the Cookie Cutter tool from the toolbox. Then, select a shape from the Shape library in the Options bar; if you don't see the shape you want to use, click the triangle on the right side of the library and choose a different library of shapes.

Click the triangle next to Shape Options in the Options bar, and then choose any size and proportion restrictions you want to impose. If you select Unconstrained, you can size and skew the shape however you want.

> **T I P**
>
> **See the Shapes.** By default, Photoshop Elements displays the shapes as small thumbnails. Those of us with older eyes may have an easier time with larger thumbnails. Click the triangle at the right side of the library, and then choose Large Thumbnail. Choose Large List to see the name of the shape with its thumbnail.

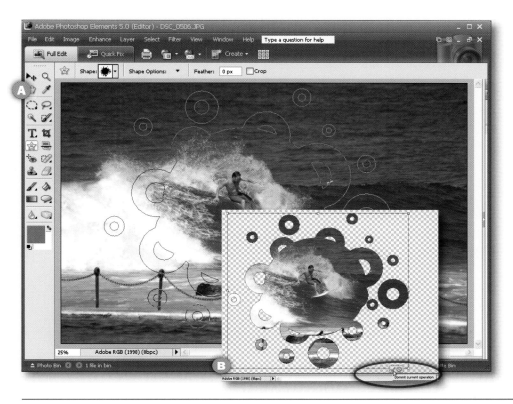

2. Crop the Image.

Drag the Cookie Cutter tool over the area of the image **A** that you want to keep. To keep the shape proportional, press the Shift key as you draw; to move the shape around on the screen, press the spacebar. You can also reposition the crop border after you've drawn the shape, which appears in the layer in the Layers palette. Drag the edges of the shape to encompass more or less of the image. When the shape is where you want it, click the Commit button below the selection or press Enter to apply the crop **B**.

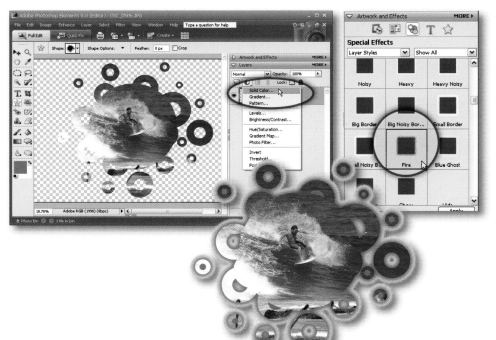

3. Provide a Background.

The interesting shape will show up better on a background, so we'll add one using an adjustment layer. In the Layers palette, click the Create Adjustment Layer icon, and then choose Solid Color. Select a color from the color picker, and click OK. Then, in the Layers palette, drag the adjustment layer below the layer with your cropped image.

To really set off your border, apply a layer style: select the image layer, and then select a layer style from the Special Effects palette. We used Fire for a neat effect. ▦

Cropping and Straightening

Crop and straighten an image at the same time, using any of these methods.

The Straighten Tool

Mike McHugh, Wayne Rankin, and Jack Davis look a bit off in this image, with a horizon that isn't quite horizontal. Luckily, the Straighten tool makes it pretty easy to fix a crooked horizon line.

1. Select the Straighten tool.

2. Choose a canvas option.

If you select Crop to Remove Background, you'll lose some of your image; if you select Grow Canvas to Fit Rotated Image, you'll have extra white space; and if you select Crop to Original Size, you'll have some extra area you might want to fill in. We'll choose Crop to Remove Background because we can afford to lose a bit of this background.

3. Click at one point of the horizon line and drag along it **A**. When you release it, the Straighten tool crops and straightens the image at the same time **B**. The horizon line makes it easy to see how the image should be aligned, but you can use any line that should be horizontal.

The Crop Tool

Working with the same image, we can use the Crop tool to crop and straighten it.

1. Select the Crop tool.

2. Select No Restriction for the aspect ratio. When you select No Restriction, you can rotate the image.

3. Select the area **A** you want to include in the final image, and then move the cursor outside the selection area until you see curved arrows **B**. Then, rotate the image so that the horizon is horizontal. Click the Commit icon or double-click in the area to confirm the change.

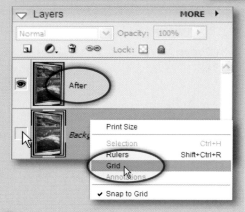

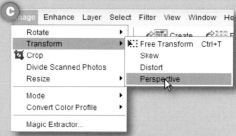

The Grid

Sometimes it's a bit trickier to correct the angles of an image. When you need to adjust both vertical and horizontal lines, use the grid. We'll use the grid to adjust this photo of a painting, which was taken at an angle to avoid glare from the glass.

1. Start with the vertical lines. Select the Crop tool, and select No Restriction for the aspect ratio. Click and drag an area to crop **A**. Move the cursor away from the image, so that it becomes a rotation cursor, and then line it up to make the edges of the image vertical **B**. Click the Commit icon to straighten and crop at the same time.

2. Press Ctrl+Alt+J to duplicate the background layer so that the original remains intact. Name the new layer "After."

3. Choose View > Grid to display a grid over the image so that you have a guide for alignment.

4. Select the After layer, and then choose Image > Transform > Perspective **C**. Select the top-right corner handle and drag it up until the image looks square with the grid **D**. You may also need to pull the side handle so that the bottom of the image looks correct, too. Manipulate the handles to minimize the distortion. When it looks right, click the Commit icon or double-click the image to apply the perspective changes.

5. Crop the revised image **E**: Drag the Rectangular Marquee tool to define the new edges, and then choose Image > Crop. Or use the Crop tool to crop the image. 🕮

Correcting Distortion

Shift your perspective with the Correct Camera Distortion filter. Several options and a handy grid let you correct the effects of lens distortion and awkward angles.

1. Duplicate the Background Layer.

Jack Davis took this great photo of the San Diego Museum of Modern Art, but the perspective is a bit dodgy. We're going to be making some radical changes to this image, so let's make sure the original pixels remain intact. Press Ctrl+J to copy the background layer. Name the new layer "Remove Distortion."

2. Apply the Filter.

Choose Filter > Correct Camera Distortion. The filter's dialog box displays a large preview of the image with a grid overlay. That grid makes our job a lot easier. If the grid doesn't show up well over your image, click the Color box and select a new color for it.

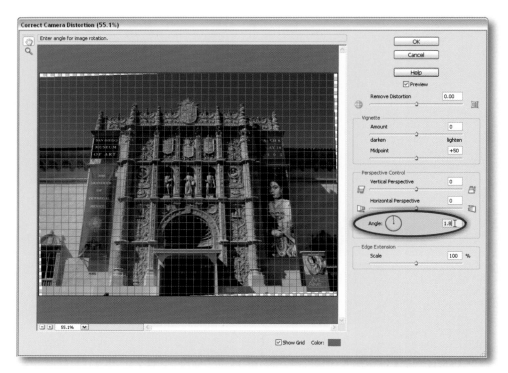

3. Adjust the Angle.

The grid lines make it clear that the building in this image is falling away to the right. We'll use the Angle setting to correct that. Click the line in the angle circle and drag it to the appropriate angle. Identify a horizontal line in the image, such as the roof of a building, and then adjust the angle until that line aligns with a horizontal line in the grid. To align the museum in this image, we need to move the angle to the left.

> **T I P**
>
> **Angle Control.** It can be tricky to drag the angle line smoothly. Click the line close to the circle's edge and drag it slowly for more control of the angle movement. For even finer control, select the Angle field and press the up and down arrow keys to nudge it slightly.

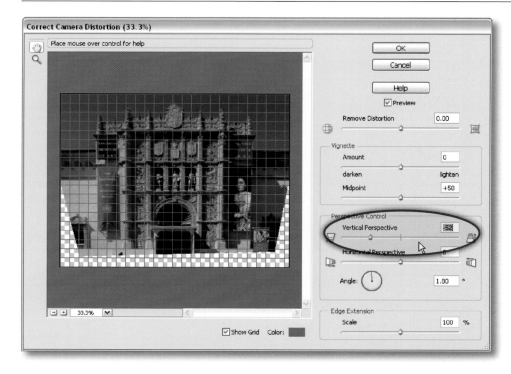

4. Correct the Perspective.

In this image, it's the vertical perspective that concerns us, but you can adjust horizontal perspective using this filter, too. Drag the Vertical Perspective slider to the left to tilt the image downward, which expands the top of the image and contracts the bottom. The vertical lines in the image should parallel the vertical lines in the grid; we're using the pillars in this building as our vertical lines. You can nudge the perspective value using the up and down keys.

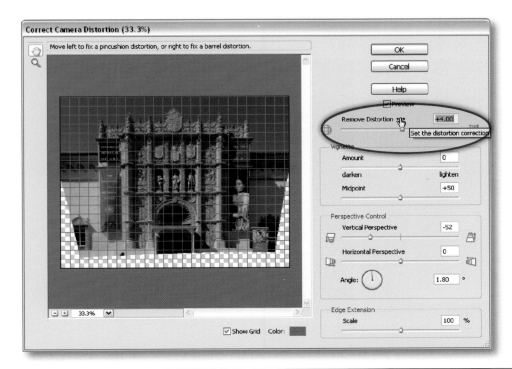

5. Remove Curved Distortion.

Lens barrel, or pincushion, distortion, can make an image appear bloated or too thin in the middle. The Remove Distortion option straightens horizontal or vertical lines that bend away from or toward the center of the image. Move the Remove Distortion slider to the left to expand the center or to the right to contract it. This effect can be dramatic; be careful not to go too far.

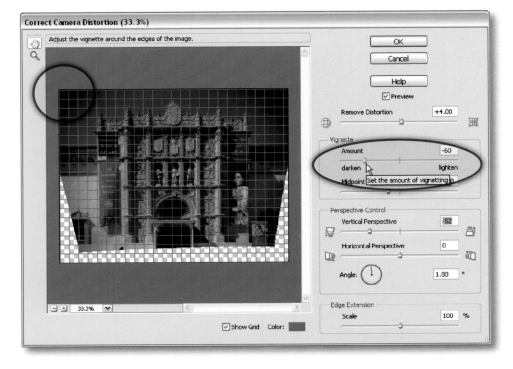

6. Select Vignette Options.

If the edges of the image are inappropriately dark, a common lens distortion problem, use the Vignette option to lighten it. You can also use this option to darken the edges for a more dramatic look. Move the Amount slider to the left to darken the edges, or to the right to lighten them. The Midpoint slider determines the width of the area affected by the Amount slider; move it to the right to restrict the effect to the edges of the image.

Click OK when you're satisfied with the image.

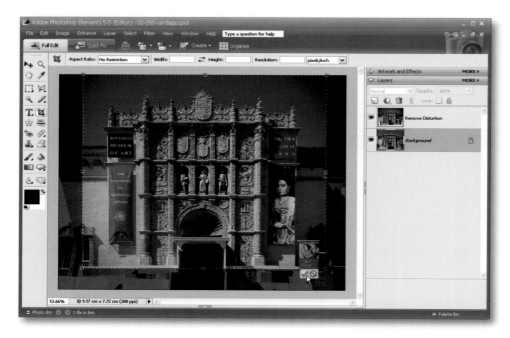

7. Crop the Image.

When we change perspective and angle, or remove curved distortion, the edges of the image change. To tidy the image, we'll crop it. Select the Crop tool, drag it over the final image area, and release the mouse. You can adjust the crop area by dragging a corner. To accept the crop, click the check mark icon. ▥

Fixing Images Quickly

Change lighting and color attributes to quickly improve the appearance of a photo.

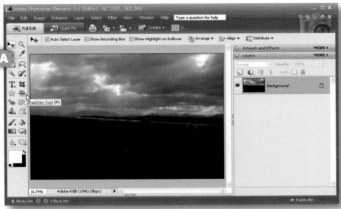

1. Fix the Horizon Line.

Select the image in the Organizer, and then choose Edit > Go to Standard Edit. We'll start there to correct the horizon line before going to the Quick Fix workspace. Select the Straighten tool, select Crop to Remove Background in the Options bar, and then drag a line along the horizon **A**. Photoshop Elements aligns the horizon and crops the image at the same time **B**.

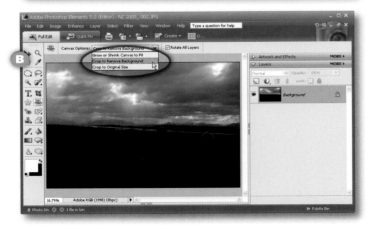

2. Open the Quick Fix Workspace.

Now we're ready to take advantage of the Quick Fix tools. Click Quick Fix to switch to the Quick Fix workspace. To easily see the changes you make, choose Before and After from the View menu. Use the Hand tool to pan the image, if you need to, so that you're seeing the area of the image you're most interested in.

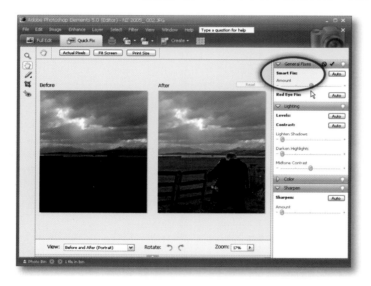

3. Apply Smart Fix.

Smart Fix corrects the overall color balance for an image, and it can also improve shadow and highlight detail. Click Auto to let Photoshop Elements apply Smart Fix to your image, or move the Amount slider to adjust how much Smart Fix alters the photo. If you try the Auto setting and don't like it, click Reset to return to the original settings.

4. Adjust the Lighting.

This image is backlit, and there are dark areas in the foreground. Drag the Lighten Shadows slider to reveal more detail in the shadows. Adjust the Darken Highlights slider to reveal more detail in the lighter areas of the image. Adjust the Midtone Contrast slider to change the contrast of the middle tones. For this image, we won't move the Midtone Contrast slider at all because increasing the midtone contrast darkens the faces too much, and decreasing it loses detail in the grass.

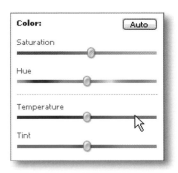

5. Adjust the Color.

Quickly adjust the color of the image using the Color options. The Saturation slider determines how saturated the colors are. The Hue slider changes the colors themselves, and the Temperature slider determines how warm or cool the colors are. If there's a color cast on the image, use the Hue and Temperature sliders to remove it.

6. Sharpen the Image Carefully.

A small amount of sharpening goes a long way, and usually gives better results than more aggressive sharpening. Usually, you'll get the best results if you move the slider slightly to the right. You want to sharpen the image enough that it's clear, but not so much that the edges dominate.

7. Save the Image.

When you're happy with the image, save it. Choose File > Save As, and save it with a different name. To keep the original handy with it, select Save in Version Set with Original. When you save in a version set, you can access every version of an image easily in the Organizer. ▦

Understanding Levels

Get to know one of the most versatile features in Photoshop Elements: the Levels dialog box. You can achieve professional results using the Levels dialog box to adjust brightness and contrast, create masks, and add special effects.

Accessing the Levels Dialog Box

There are several ways to open the Levels dialog box, but we recommend that you always create a Levels adjustment layer, so that you can edit the levels without affecting the original image. To add an adjustment layer, click the Create Adjustment Layer icon in the Layers palette and then choose Levels. You'll see the same dialog box if you choose Enhance > Auto Levels or Enhance > Adjust Lighting > Levels.

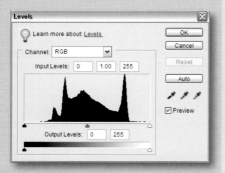

The Histogram

The mysterious-looking bar chart in the center of the dialog box, called a histogram, indicates which brightness levels are present in the image, and how prevalent each shade is. The histogram displays tonal distribution from black to white. Beneath the histogram are three sliders, which set the black point, the white point, and the midpoint. Move the black point slider to change the point at which shades become completely black; move the white point slider to change the point at which shades become completely white. The midpoint slider controls the overall brightness of the image by brightening or darkening all the shades between black and white without changing the extremes.

The Gradient

The gradient at the bottom of the dialog box shows all the shades that could be in your image, from the darkest colors to the brightest colors. Using the Output slider, you can determine how dark the dark colors can be, or how light the light colors can be.

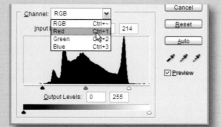

Channels

You can make adjustments to the entire image or to individual channels: Red, Blue, or Green. Choose a channel from the Channels menu. Making adjustments to an individual channel gives you greater control over how bright or dark a particular set of colors is. █

Adjusting Lighting in Photos

Unless you're taking photos in ideal lighting conditions, you'll probably want to touch up the shadows and highlights.

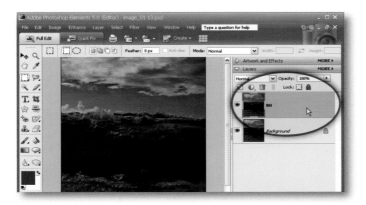

1. Duplicate the Layer.

There's no Shadows/Highlights adjustment layer in Photoshop Elements, so, to keep our original intact, we'll make changes to a duplicate layer. Press Ctrl+Alt+J, and name the layer "Shadows/Highlights." You can hide the background layer, if you like, as we make changes to the Shadows/Highlights layer.

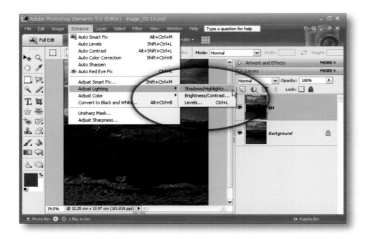

2. Open the Shadows/Highlights Dialog Box.

Choose Enhanced > Adjust Lighting > Shadows/Highlights. Photoshop Elements displays the Shadows/Highlight dialog box and automatically applies default settings. Let's move all the settings to 0 so that we can see the original we're working with.

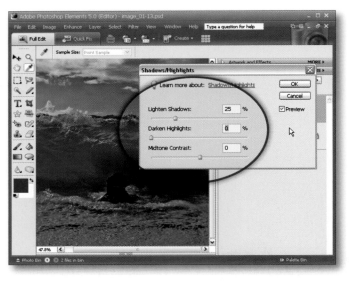

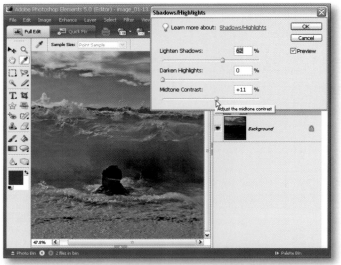

3. Make Adjustments.

Move the Lighten Shadows slider to bring out the detail in the darker areas of your image. Moving this slider even 1% or 2% can make a dramatic difference, without changing the mood of your image. Moving the slider all the way to the right removes all the shadows.

Move the Darken Highlights slider to bring out detail in the brighter areas of your image. In an underexposed image, you don't need to darken the highlights, but in an overexposed image, darken the highlights to see the detail that lurks there.

Move the Midtone Contrast slider if lightening the shadows flattened the image. This slider increases the contrast in the midtones, without affecting the darkest and brightest areas of the photo. To make fine adjustments, click in the field and then tap the arrow keys on your keyboard. ▦

Removing Color Casts

A color cast is an unwanted color shift, often the result of lighting conditions, an inappropriate camera setting, or scanning a faded photo. For example, we'd like to remove this unhealthy yellow color from Jack Davis's skin in this photo. Use one of these five methods to remove color casts in Photoshop Elements.

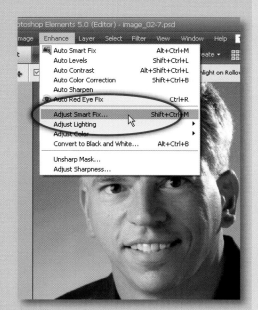

Auto Smart Fix

Choose Enhance > Auto Smart Fix. This is the fastest way to remove a color cast, but you have no control over the settings. Photoshop Elements uses standard settings to reduce the color cast. For a little more control, choose Enhance > Adjust Smart Fix. In this dialog box, you can adjust the amount of Smart Fix that Photoshop Elements applies.

> ### T I P
>
> **Same Smart Fix.** The Auto Smart Fix command in the Standard Edit workspace performs the same action as the Auto option in the Smart Fix section of the settings in the Quick Fix workspace. Likewise, the Amount slider in the Adjust Smart Fix dialog box acts just like the Amount slider in the Quick Fix workspace.

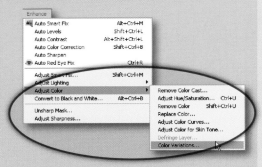

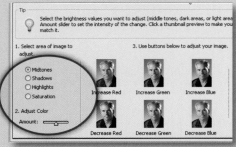

Variations

Choose Enhance > Adjust Color > Color Variations to open the Color Variations dialog box. There are several options in this dialog box. Photoshop Elements automatically applies default adjustments, but you can move the sliders to change each setting. First, select the area of the image you want to adjust: shadows, highlights, midtones, or color saturation. Then, click Decrease Red or Decrease Green or Decrease Blue to remove a color cast, depending on the image. For this example, we'll click Decrease Red multiple times and then click Decrease Green once, as well. You may need to make changes to the shadows, highlights, and midtones to get just the right color.

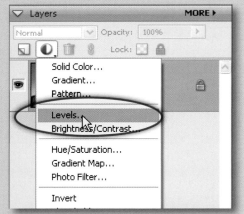

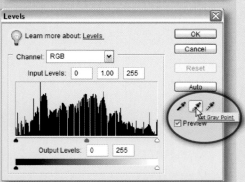

Levels

Select the layer in the Layers palette. Then select the Create Adjustment Layer icon and choose Levels. To remove a color cast, we don't need to move any sliders in the Levels dialog box. Instead, we'll use the Set Gray Point eyedropper. Select the Set Gray Point eyedropper, and then click an area of the image that is a neutral gray. In this image, we'll select an area of Jack's hair. (Gray hair has its advantages.) The color of the image changes automatically as you click. You may need to click a few different areas to get the look you want.

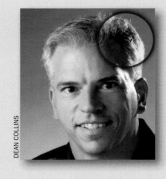

DEAN COLLINS

Remove Color Cast

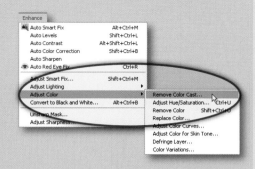

Of course, you could just choose Enhance > Adjust Color > Remove Color Cast. The Remove Color Cast dialog box uses just one eyedropper, and it's already selected when the dialog box is open. Just click anywhere on the image that is a neutral gray, white, or black, and Photoshop Elements will adjust the color of the image accordingly. This is the easiest way to remove a color cast accurately.

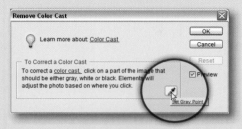

Adjust Skin Tone

When a photo contains people, the most important color to get right is the skin tone. Choose Enhance > Adjust Color > Adjust Color for Skin Tone A. In the Adjust Color for Skin Tone dialog box, click any person's skin in the photo B. Photoshop Elements automatically adjusts the skin color and the rest of the color in the image accordingly. To make further adjustments, move the Tan and Blush sliders, or adjust the ambient light temperature. In this image of Jack, the ambient light makes the most difference. ▥

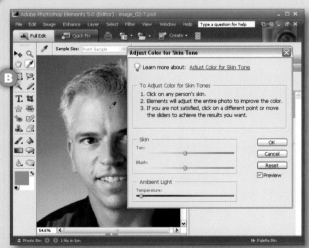

Reducing Noise

Remove unwanted noise, including JPEG artifacts, from your photos, including those taken with cell phones.

1. Duplicate the Layer.

Photoshop Elements can't help us lower the noise level from a young child, but it can remove much of the noise from her photo. Of course, as we often do, we'll start by duplicating the original layer, so that we can safely make changes without affecting the original. Press Ctrl+Alt+J, and name the layer "Noise Reduction."

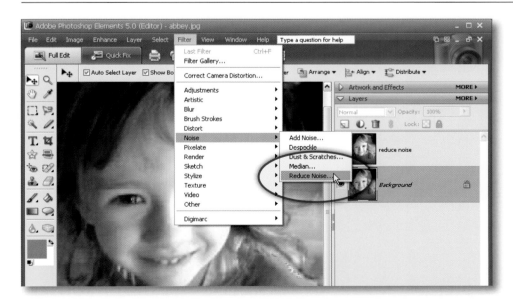

2. Apply the Reduce Noise Filter.

Choose Filter > Noise > Reduce Noise. Photoshop Elements opens the Reduce Noise dialog box with its default settings. So that we can start from scratch, drag all the sliders to 0. Then zoom in to an area of the image with noise.

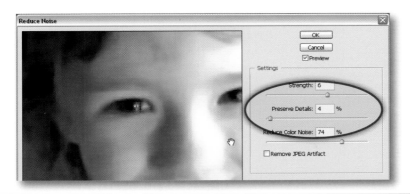

3. Adjust the Strength Slider.

The Strength slider determines how much luminance noise, which is the presence of light pixels in dark areas, is removed. As you reduce the luminance noise, you may lose some of the original detail in the image. Move the Preserve Detail slider to keep more of the detail. You may need to move both the Strength and the Preserve Detail sliders a few times to find the right balance.

4. Reduce Color Noise.

Stray bits of color that appear in an image are called color noise. Move the Reduce Color Noise slider to the right until most of the color noise is gone.

5. Remove JPEG Artifacts.

Select Remove JPEG Artifacts to get rid of blocky artifacts and halos that may appear in JPEG images that were saved with low-quality settings. You may be lucky enough to remove all the JPEG artifacts using the Strength and Preserve Details sliders, but if any remain, select Remove JPEG Artifacts.

6. Sharpen the Image.

Removing noise can leave your image a little blurred. It's often a good idea to sharpen the image after removing noise. Choose Enhance > Auto Sharpen to sharpen up the edges a little bit. ▥

Color Curves

Improve color tones in an image by adjusting highlights, midtones, and shadows.

1. Duplicate the Layer.

We'll be using the Adjust Color Curves feature, new in Photoshop Elements 5, to improve the color tones in an image. Despite its name, the Adjust Color Curves feature does not create an adjustment layer. So, to preserve the original, we'll make changes to a duplicate layer. Press Ctrl+Alt+J and name the layer "Adjust Color Curves."

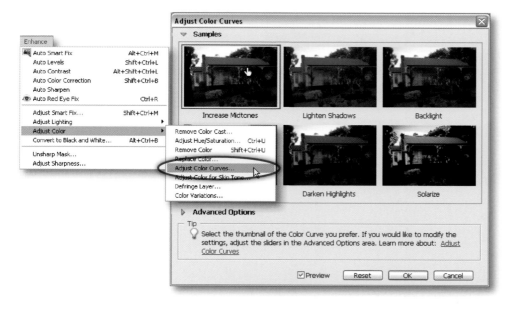

2. Adjust the Color Curves.

Choose Enhance > Adjust Color > Adjust Color Curves. The Adjust Color Curves dialog box displays six thumbnails of the image, each the result of a different adjustment. Make sure Preview is selected in the dialog box, and then click each sample to see its effect on your photo. It's handy to use one of the samples as a starting point. Select the one that comes closest to the results you want.

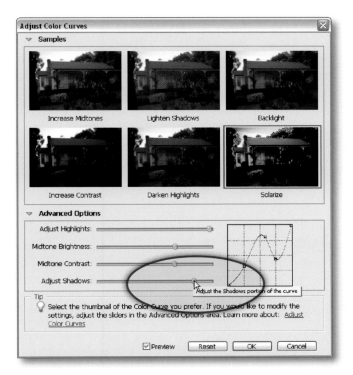

3. Fine-tune the Curve Settings.

Click the triangle next to Advanced Options to reveal sliders. You can fine-tune the highlights to lighten or darken them, adjust the midtone brightness, increase or decrease the midtone contrast, and lighten or darken the shadows. As you move each slider, the curve changes to reflect the new value. When you have the look you want, click OK. ▥

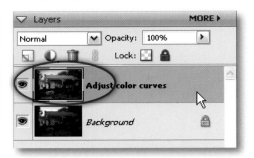

About Sharpening

Sharpening an image defines its edges more clearly. Most images benefit from a small amount of sharpening, but apply it in moderation: if you sharpen too much, you can emphasize noise and other artifacts in the image. Keep in mind how you'll be using the image. Printed images may need a different amount of sharpening than images displayed on the web.

Sharpening affects the pixels of an image. To leave the originals untouched, create a copy of the background layer and sharpen that layer.

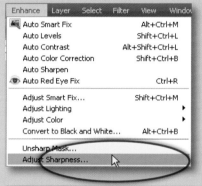

T I P

Clarity, Not Noise. Reduce the noise before you sharpen the image, so that sharpening doesn't make the noise more pronounced.

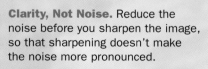

Adjust Sharpness

New to Photoshop Elements 5.0, you can fine-tune the sharpening settings. Choose Enhance > Adjust Sharpness. Then, drag the sliders to adjust the sharpening in the image. Photoshop Elements uses the settings in this dialog box when you apply the Auto Sharpen command.

Make sure Preview is selected; as you make changes, you'll see their effect in the preview window. Click the + or – button to zoom in and out; drag the image to see a different area.

Amount determines how much the image is sharpened. Drag the slider to the right to increase the contrast between edge pixels; drag it to the left to decrease the contrast.

Radius determines how far from an edge the pixels are sharpened. Sharpening is more obvious when you increase the radius. In fact, if you increase it too much, a halo starts to appear around the image. We recommend keeping the Radius value low for most images.

Remove determines which sharpening algorithm is used. Gaussian Blur is the default. Lens Blur can reduce sharpening halos and result in finer sharpening of detail. Motion Blur reduces the effects of blur that occurs when the camera or the subject of the photograph moves. (If you choose Motion Blur, specify the angle of the blur.)

The More Refined option processes the file more slowly to remove the blurring more accurately, but it can also make digital noise more obvious. We often deselect More Refined to reduce the noise a bit.

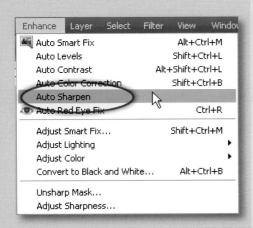

Auto Sharpen

To sharpen an image using the default settings, choose Enhance > Auto Sharpen. Photoshop Elements sharpens the image automatically.

The Auto Sharpen command applies the values last used in the Adjust Sharpness dialog box. If you usually use the same settings to sharpen an image, choose those settings in the Adjust Sharpness dialog box, and then use Auto Sharpen to quickly apply them.

Unsharp Mask

The Unsharp Mask filter is the most advanced sharpening option. It evaluates the differences between pixels, and, depending on the threshold you specify, increases the pixels' contrast to reduce blur. Lighter pixels get lighter, and darker pixels get darker. The effects of the filter are much more dramatic on screen than in high-resolution printing. If you're planning to print the image, experiment to find out what settings work best.

Choose Enhance > Unsharp Mask. Make sure Preview is selected so you can see how the settings affect your image.

Amount determines how much to increase the contrast. If you're planning to print at a high resolution, try a value between 150% and 200%.

Radius specifies how many pixels to sharpen around edges. A lower value sharpens only the edge pixels. For high-resolution images, try a radius between 1 and 2.

Threshold determines which pixels get sharpened. The threshold specifies how far pixels must be from the surrounding area to be considered edge pixels. The default Threshold value is 0, which sharpens all pixels in an image. To prevent additional noise in most images, experiment with Threshold values between 2 and 20. ▦

INSIGHT

Insight: Sharpening in Quick Fix Mode. The main sharpening tools are available only in the Full Edit mode, but you can also apply some sharpening in Quick Fix mode, as we did in "Reducing Noise."

Adjusting Hue and Saturation

Adjust the color quality in your images to bring more life to photos.

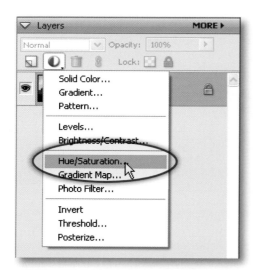

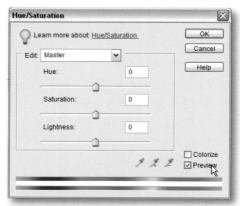

1. Create an Adjustment Layer.

Click the Create Adjustment Layer icon, and then choose Hue/Saturation.

You could adjust Hue and Saturation by choosing Enhance > Adjust Color > Adjust Hue/Saturation, but using an adjustment layer lets us experiment with color changes without permanently altering the original layer.

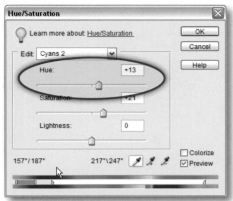

2. Adjust the Hue.

You can tweak the hue for the entire image by moving the Hue slider. To change the hue for only one color or group of colors, choose a color group from the Edit menu. For example, to change only the reds, choose Reds from the Edit menu.

The colors you're working with are marked in the gradient at the bottom of the dialog box. Drag the slider to select different colors in the gradient, to narrow the range, or to expand the range of colors. You can use the eyedropper to select a particular color in your image to work with, and then adjust the range in the gradient. For example, you can make the grain in this image more golden by moving the red colors into a yellow hue, and adjust the hue of the sky to darken the color a bit.

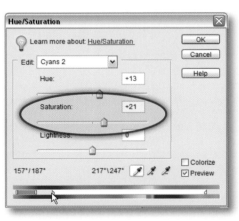

3. Adjust the Saturation.

The Saturation slider makes colors more or less vivid. You can adjust the saturation for the entire image, or for a particular color range. For example, you might want to make a vivid background color less distracting. Or, as in this image, you could increase the saturation of the blues to make the sky color more intense.

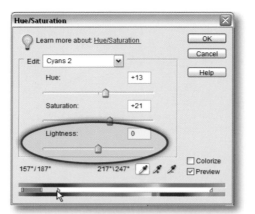

4. Adjust the Lightness.

The Lightness slider reduces the overall tonal range to lighten or darken part of an image. It's best not to use this slider on the entire image, but instead on a particular range of colors.

5. Mask Part of the Image.

If there's an area of the image you want to leave unaffected by the adjustment layer, mask it. In this image, we'd like to keep the barn in its original color, so that changes to hue, saturation, and lighting don't affect it. To mask the barn, select the Paintbrush tool, set black as the foreground color in the toolbox, and then paint over the barn. The masked area appears in the adjustment layer in the Layers palette, and it is not affected by any adjustments.

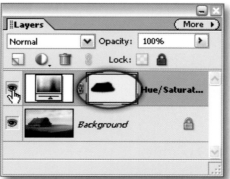

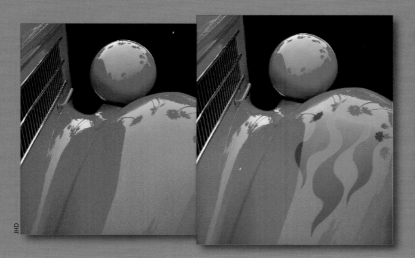

Adding an Object to a Photo

Why limit yourself to reality? Use Photoshop Elements to add sizzle, such as a flame on the hood of a classy car.

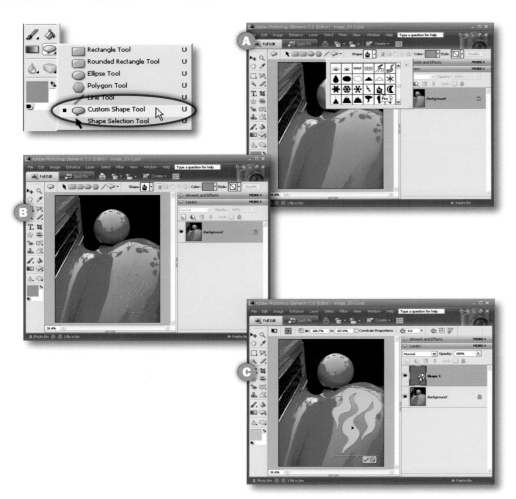

1. Draw a Shape.

Select the Custom Shape tool, and then select a shape from the Shape menu. If the shape you want isn't there **A**, click the triangle and choose a set of shapes to view. We'll choose Nature, and then select the fire.

Drag the tool to draw the shape **B**; press the Shift key as you draw if you want to keep the shape proportional. Photoshop Elements automatically creates a new layer for the shape. Use the Move tool to resize, position, and rotate the shape. Don't worry about the color **C**.

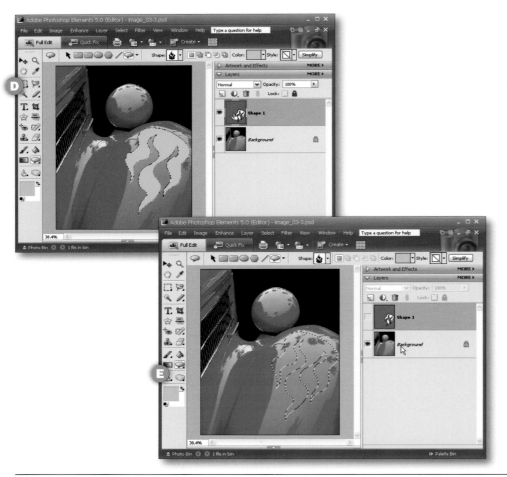

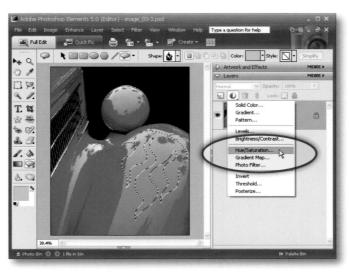

2. Load a Selection.

We're going to use this layer to create a selection. Press the Ctrl key while you select the shape layer **D**. The shape is now a selection. Hide the shape layer. You can even delete the shape layer if you want to, and the selection will remain **E**.

3. Add an Adjustment Layer.

Click the Create Adjustment Layer icon, and choose Hue/Saturation. Photoshop Elements creates a Hue/Saturation adjustment layer with everything but the selection masked. Changes you make to hue and saturation will affect only the selection.

You won't see the selection border on the image, but it's still there.

4. Colorize the Selection.
Select Colorize in the Hue/Saturation dialog box. Then, move the Hue and Saturation sliders to get the color you want. Because we want the flame to have an airbrushed effect, we won't move the Lightness slider. When the selection is the color you want, click OK to close the dialog box.

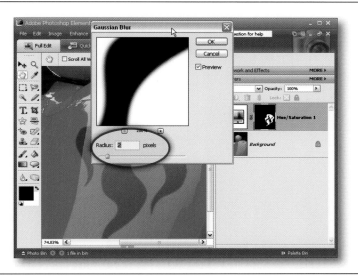

5. Soften the Edge.
We'll add a slight blur to soften the edges of the flame. Zoom in to be able to see it. Then, choose Filter > Blur > Gaussian Blur. Set the blur for about 2 pixels to get an attractive, airbrushed look.

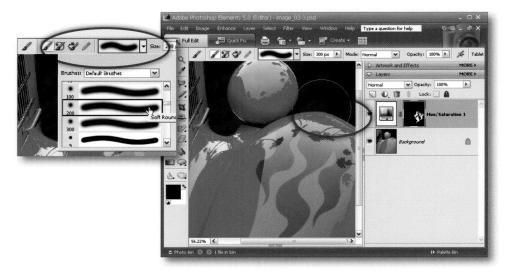

6. Fade the Edge.
We want the flames to have a more organic origin, so we'll fade the bottom edge a bit. Remember that the selection is the only thing in the adjustment layer that isn't masked. Select the adjustment layer. Then, use the Paintbrush tool (with black as the foreground color) to paint over the edge of the selection, extending the mask a little bit. You may want to reduce the opacity of the brush so that the flames gradually fade into the car. ▥

3

PHOTO RETOUCHING

Refine Images, Resuscitate Memories, and Enhance Your Photos Like a True Professional

WE WERE ABSOLUTELY CERTAIN that Chapter 2 was going to be the most useful and interesting chapter of all. However, it seems we grossly underestimated the fantastic stuff contained within the sublime pages of Chapter 3. From now on, we will not make such outrageous claims. Chapter 3 shows you how to make the world in your images a better place with techniques to retouch and enhance less-than-perfect photographs.

None of Us Are Perfect

As mentioned above, we all make mistakes. And, of course, none of us are physically flawless either, especially not your humble authors. So it brings us great comfort to know that, though we cannot help you remember to buy milk on the way home, we can help you reduce wrinkles and blemishes, whiten teeth, and remove red eyes. In fact, the Liquify filter builds muscles much more quickly than a steady weight-lifting routine. If only Photoshop Elements could do for our physical bodies what it does for our digital images, we'd be golden.

A Sharper Image

Even a shot that is in perfect focus can benefit from sharpening. Or you may need to replace one sky with another for dramatic effect. You can even remove people or other objects that clutter up a photo. The techniques for refining your images, developed by Jack Davis and well-proven in Photoshop and Photoshop Elements, improve just about any image you work with. Jack's philosophy of "quality, flexibility, and speed" comes through in these techniques, giving you fast, reliable ways to turn a good photograph into a great one.

What Is Old Is New Again

Rediscovering old treasures can be even more rewarding than working with new images. Torn corners, faded colors, creases, and stains are no match for the toolset in Photoshop Elements. We'll walk through a photo restoration project together, moving from the scanned image of a well-worn photo to a cleaned-up, restored, and still appropriately nostalgic digital image. In our example, we use a photo of Mike's father receiving an award from an athletic hero, but you can use the same process to recover photos of grandparents, historical figures, or buildings.

Removing Red Eye

Quickly replace the unfortunate red highlight in a photo with realistic eye color.

1. Zoom In on the Eyes.

Red eye is a common problem in flash photography. When the light from the flash reflects off the back of the iris, the subject's eyes appear red. To replace the red color with a more accurate eye color, first use the Zoom tool to zoom in on the eyes.

2. Select the Red Eye Removal Tool.

This problem is so common that Photoshop Elements has a tool specifically designed for it. Select the Red Eye Removal tool in the toolbox. It's easy to find because it looks like a red eye!

3. Set the Options.

In the Options bar, set the Pupil Size and Darken Amount values. The pupil size is the proportion of pupil to the entire eye area; the default is 50%, and that's a good place to start. The darken amount determines how dark or light the pupil itself should be: 100% creates a deep black pupil, and smaller percentages create lighter pupils.

4. Apply the Red Eye Removal Tool.

Drag the Red Eye Removal tool over the eyes. Photoshop Elements detects the red eye and applies the settings you chose in the Options bar.

If it doesn't look quite right, press Ctrl+Z to undo, and then change the settings and drag the tool again. ▥

INSIGHT

Which Way to Fix Red Eyes? There are several ways to fix red eyes in Photoshop Elements. We showed you our favorite method here, but you can experiment with other options as well.

- To let Photoshop Elements automatically fix any red eyes it detects, select Automatically Fix Red Eyes when you import images into the Organizer. This is a quick, automatic option, but it gives you no control. And sometimes it doesn't even find the red eyes.

- In the Editor, choose Enhance > Auto Red Eye Fix to let Photoshop Elements detect the red eyes and fix them automatically. Again, you have no control, and Photoshop

Elements sometimes fails to detect the red eyes. However, if it works, it's a quick option. Remember that you can press Ctrl+Z to undo the command.

- After you select the Red Eye Removal tool, you can click Auto in the Options bar. Photoshop Elements attempts to find and fix the red eyes without you dragging the tool.

We prefer using the Red Eye Removal tool to set options and drag the tool over the eyes because it gives us more control. Also, we know that we can find the red eyes, even if Photoshop Elements isn't always able to detect them.

Fixing Blemishes and Wrinkles

Use Photoshop Elements to reverse the marks of time. Several tools help you reduce wrinkles and blemishes.

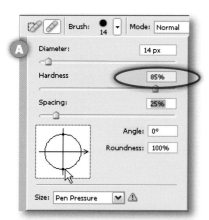

1. Set Up the Healing Brush Tool.

We'll use the Healing Brush tool to reduce the wrinkles and blemishes in an image. First, duplicate the layer (Ctrl+Alt+J) to preserve the original pixels. Name the new layer Remove blemishes. Then, select the Healing Brush tool in the toolbox.

In the Options bar, set up a fairly small, hard brush. We'll use an 85% hard brush **A**, but you may need to change the softness to match the focus of the image you're working with. We'll make the brush elliptical, with a 45-degree angle **B**, so that the changes we make will be more subtle. Finally, increase the spacing so that gaps in the brush stroke create a random edge, making it harder to see that we've touched up the image.

Don't select the Aligned option **C**; we don't want the Healing Brush tool to repeat patterns.

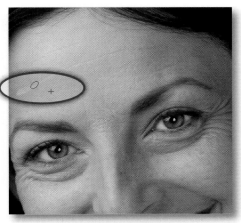

2. Paint Out Wrinkles.

Let's tackle the wrinkles first. Zoom in to see them clearly. Then, press the Alt key and click in an unwrinkled area to select the source point. Now, paint over the wrinkle. Each time you click and drag, you start over from the source point.

You can quickly improve someone's appearance by painting over wrinkles under the eyes. Use the Healing Brush tool to paint over obvious blemishes as well.

3. Remove Spots.

We'll switch now to the Spot Healing Brush tool. Select the tool, and set a brush size close to the size of the spot you want to remove. Then, simply click the spot to remove it. Unlike the standard Healing Brush tool, the Spot tool doesn't require you to set a source point. Use the Spot Healing Brush tool to remove all the small spots in the image. You can also use it to remove some wrinkles.

T I P

Seeing in the Dark. If you have trouble seeing all the spots on dark clothes or background areas, use an adjustment layer to exaggerate the spots. Create a Levels adjustment layer, and then move the midtones until you clearly see the problem areas. When you've removed the spots, delete the adjustment layer.

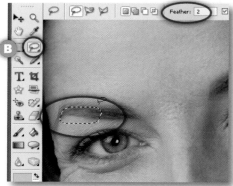

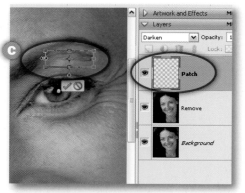

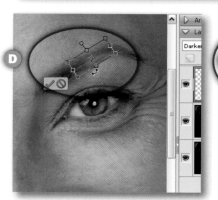

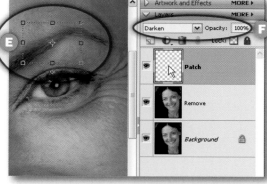

4. Patch Problem Areas.

Some problems are easier to fix by "borrowing" from another area of the image **A**, especially if you want to make the features more symmetrical. We'll patch the thin eyebrow in this image, so that the eyebrows match. First, zoom in to the area around the eyes. Use the Lasso tool to select a full area in the left eyebrow, and give it a 2-pixel feather in the Options bar **B**. Then press Ctrl+C to copy the selection, and press Ctrl+V to paste it. Photoshop Elements creates a new layer for the pasted object **C**.

Make sure Auto Select Layer is deselected, and move the patch to the right eyebrow **C**. It's pointing in the wrong direction, so we'll need to flip it over. Choose Image > Rotate > Flip Layer Horizontal **D**. Then, press Ctrl+T to open Free Transform mode, and rotate the layer so that it fits the eyebrow **E**. When it's in the right position, click the Commit icon or press Enter. Finally, choose the Darken blending mode **F** for the layer so that the skin beneath the eyebrow matches the surrounding area. You may also need to change the opacity of the layer.

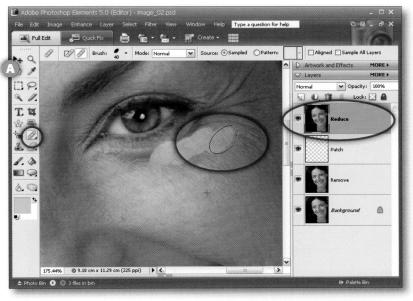

5. Soften Fine Lines and Wrinkles.

Now, we'll move into the detail work. First, let's duplicate everything we've done so far on a new layer **A**. Select the top layer, and press Alt+Shift while you type NE. (Ctrl+Alt+Shift+N is the shortcut for creating a new layer without seeing the New Layer dialog box, and Ctrl+Alt+Shift+E is the shortcut for merging visible items.) Name the layer Reduce.

Zoom in to the area around the eyes, and then select the Healing Brush tool. Press Alt and click to create a source point. Paint over the wrinkles that are near the eyes, completely removing all the wrinkles. Of course, removing all a person's wrinkles leaves a mannequin, so after you've removed the wrinkles, change the opacity of the layer **B** to 60%. The wrinkles reappear, softer than they were originally. Alternatively, you can apply the Lighten blending mode to the layer to recover a softened version of the wrinkles.

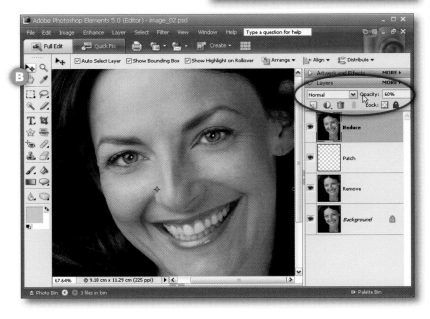

Whitening Teeth and Eyes

Make teeth sparkle and remove the bloodshot appearance in the whites of your subject's eyes.

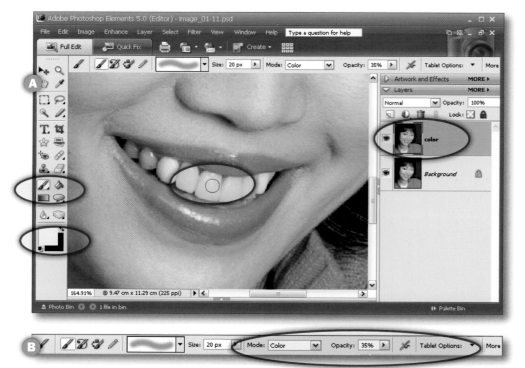

1. Remove Stains from the Teeth.

First, duplicate the layer by pressing Ctrl+Alt+J, and name the layer "Color." Then, zoom in to see the teeth **A**. Select the Paintbrush tool, and reduce its opacity to about 20–35%. Select a soft-edged **B** brush. We'll change the brush size as we work. Choose the Color blending mode to desaturate the color, so that you're taking away the stains but not adding any other color.

Make sure white is the foreground color in the toolbox, and then tap on the teeth with the toothbrush to remove stains. Press the left bracket ([) to decrease the brush size and the right bracket (]) to increase it.

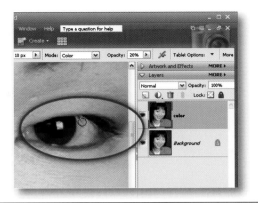

2. Clean Up the Whites of the Eyes.

Now, let's move our attention to the eyes. We'll remove the bloodshot look without adding any color. Zoom in to the eye area. Using the same Paintbrush tool you used on the teeth, with the Color blending mode and 20% opacity, click the eyes to remove the red color.

3. Brighten the White in the Eyes and Teeth.

Be a bit cautious when you brighten eyes and teeth. It's easy to overdo. Use the same brush you've been using, but apply the Soft Light blending mode, and reduce the opacity to 14%. Click the teeth to brighten them slightly, and then do the same with the whites of the eyes.

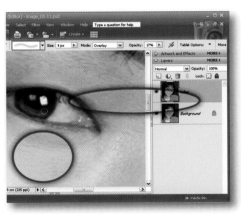

4. Brighten the Color in the Eyes.

We have just one more touch-up to perform on the eyes, in order to bring the photo to life. We'll brighten the area of the eye that is opposite from the light reflection. Choose the Overlay blending mode and an opacity of 17% for the brush, and then paint the corner of the eye opposite from the light's reflection. This slightly lighter color brings more personality to the photo. ▥

Changing Hair Color

Ever wonder what you'd look like as a redhead or a blonde? Use a gradient adjustment layer to find out, without the bother of hair dye.

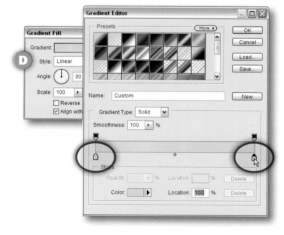

1. Create an Adjustment Layer.

Select the Create Adjustment Layer **A** icon, and choose Gradient. In the Gradient Fill **B** dialog box, click the gradient itself to open the Gradient Editor dialog box **C**. There are two color stops and two opacity stops on the gradient. Select the far-right opacity stop, and then change the Opacity value to 95%. Next, select the far-left color stop **D**, and click the color swatch at the bottom. Choose a color from the Color Picker. For this example, let's choose a yellow color, and click OK. Now, do the same thing for the other color stop, but choose a dark brown color to give contrast to the hair. Name the gradient "Hair," and then click OK. Change the angle of the gradient to match the general direction of the hair in the photo. Change the scale to adjust how quickly the gradient moves from one color to the other.

2. Blend the Layers.

At first, we're just seeing the gradient **A**. To blend it with the other layer, apply the Soft Light blending mode **B**. Now the entire image is tinted. In order to tint just the hair area, we'll need to create a mask.

Set black as the foreground color. Then press Alt+Backspace to fill the entire mask area with black. The black area in a mask is hidden, and the white area is revealed. We'll need to reveal the hair area.

Set white as the foreground color. Select the Paintbrush tool. Set the brush to Normal mode, with an opacity of 50%. Use a large brush to cover the area quickly. Paint over the hair. The gradient shows through only in the areas you're painting. You can streak the hair or paint the entire area. The mask appears in the Layers palette.

3. Adjust the Gradient.

Chances are that the color isn't quite perfect the first time. It's a simple matter now to adjust the color of the gradient. Double-click the gradient thumbnail in the Layers palette, and then double-click the gradient itself to edit it. We'll lighten both the color stops for this image, but you may want to darken the colors or choose a completely different hue. ▥

Restoring Old Photos

Rejuvenate old photographs to replace torn corners, remove creases, and correct discoloration.

1. Plan for the Project.

Old photos can be real treasures, but many have suffered over the years. Before you do anything else, scan the photo and then evaluate the scanned image to determine how best to repair it. Start with the global problems and then work your way to the details.

2. Straighten the Scanned Image.

Photographs often slip in the scanner, so scanned images are frequently skewed. Select the Straighten tool, select Crop to Original Size, and then click and drag along a horizontal edge **A**. In this image, we'll use the top of the platform as our guide. Photoshop Elements straightens the image and crops it according to the setting we chose. Small areas of black appear around parts of the border **B**, where the image shifted. We won't worry about those, because we'll be adding a new border later.

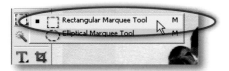

3. Fix the Color.

Scanned images present a challenge for correcting the color because the scanner background is so white or so dark that it can throw off the white point or black point for the image. To avoid this problem, start by selecting the most important area of the image using the Rectangular Marquee tool **A**. Then, create a Levels adjustment layer **B**. The adjustment layer will affect only the selected area. Click Auto in the Levels dialog box. Photoshop Elements automatically corrects the color. You can make adjustments by moving the midtones slider.

To apply the new color settings to the entire image, set white as the foreground color, and then press Alt+Backspace to fill the entire mask area with white **C**.

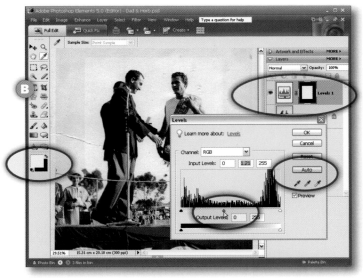

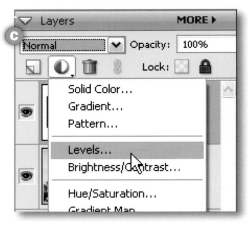

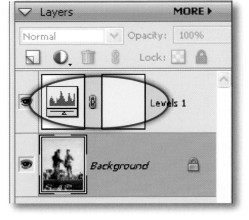

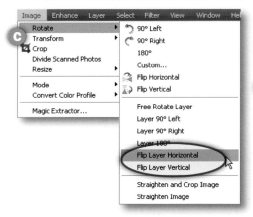

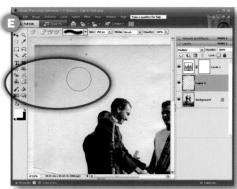

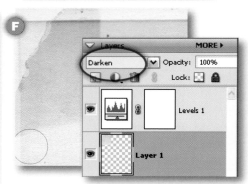

TIP

Multiply to See Beneath. For a little help aligning one layer over another, apply the Multiply blending mode temporarily. You'll be able to see both layers at once.

4. Repair the Ripped Edge.

Let's fix that ripped corner next. Duplicate the background layer by pressing Ctrl+Alt+J, and name the layer **A** "Rough Repair." It's underneath the Levels adjustment layer, so the color correction applies to both layers.

It's always best to start by working with what you have, rather than creating something from scratch. So, in this image, we'll copy an existing corner and paste it into the missing one. Use the Rectangular Marquee tool to select an area of a corner that is large enough to cover up the rip. Press Ctrl+C and then Ctrl+V to copy and paste the corner. Photoshop Elements creates a new layer for the pasted object. Use the Move tool to position the pasted corner over the ripped corner **B**.

Of course, the corner we pasted is facing the wrong direction. Choose Image > Rotate > Flip Layer Horizontal to flip the corner **C**. Shift it to the right position. You may have to rotate it slightly to fit properly. (Press Ctrl+T to access the Free Transform command **D**, and then rotate the layer. Press Enter to commit the transformation.) Apply the Darken blending mode **E** to make the new corner less obvious. Then, set up the Eraser tool with a large size and soft edge, and paint along the edge to cover the edge of the copied area **F**.

Now, merge the Rough Repair layer with the pasted object layer: Select both **G** layers and press Ctrl+E or choose Merge Layers from the Layers palette menu. Name the merged layer "Rough."

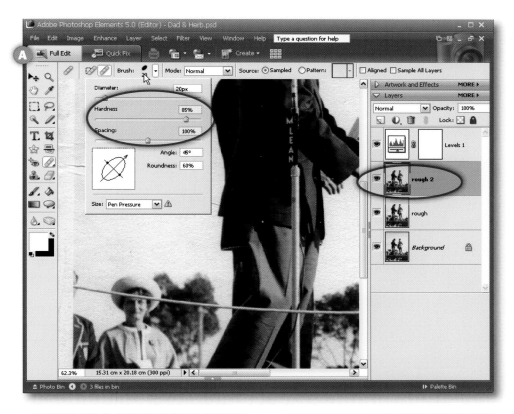

5. Retouch with the Healing Brush Tool.

We'll remove creases and other blemishes on the photo with the Healing Brush tool. First, duplicate the Rough layer **A** by pressing Ctrl+Alt+J, and name the layer "Rough 2."

Zoom in on a fold mark. Select the Healing Brush tool. Use an initial diameter of 20 pixels, 85% hardness (match the softness to the focus of the image you're working with), change the angle and roundness to an elliptical brush so that it's harder to see the changes, and increase the spacing to give a rough edge as you paint.

Press Alt and click to set a source point, and then paint along the fold **B**. The Healing Brush tool blends the change in. Use different source points to avoid repeating patterns. Paint over all the creases in the image. Paint over the ripped edge in the corner to blend it in. You can use the Healing Brush tool to clean up the larger stains as well.

INSIGHT

Border Patrol. Be careful when you use the Healing Brush tool in an area where colors contrast dramatically, such as along a shoreline or where a background meets a shirt. The Healing Brush tool includes all neighboring colors in its analysis, so it can actually pull the wrong color into the area. If you need to paint along a border, make sure that you set a source point that is right on the border. Press the Caps Lock key for more precision as you set the source point. Then paint from the border outward, from the edge to the left and then from the edge to the right.

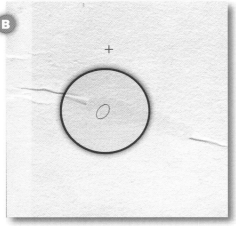

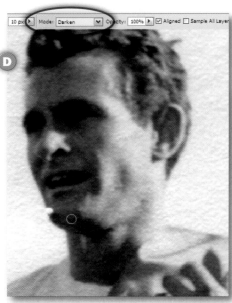

6. Touch Up Finer Details.

In this image, there's an unfortunate spot on the chin. We'll duplicate the layer (Ctrl+Alt+J) and name it "Fine Details." Then, zoom in to look at the chin. The Healing Brush tool won't work in this case, because it's a small area, but the Clone Stamp tool should do the trick. The Clone Stamp tool copies pixels from one spot to another, without attempting to blend them in.

Set up the Clone Stamp tool with a smooth edge and a large brush size. Press Alt and click a source point in the background. Paint out the spot on the background area **C**. Then change to the Darken blending mode, set a new source point on the chin **D**, and paint in the spot on the chin. This can be tricky, so you may have to adjust your brush size.

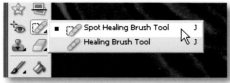

7. Remove Fine Spots.

We'll remove the random spots that still appear in this image with the Spot Healing Brush tool. Try to set the brush size to match the spot you're removing as closely as possible, and then click each spot.

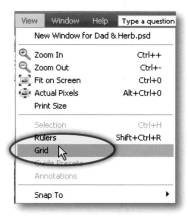

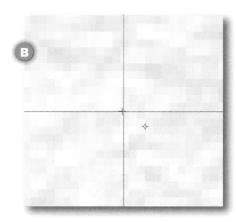

8. Create a New Border.

The old border wasn't even and square, so we'll create a new border for this image. Choose View > Grid to display the grid to use as a guide **A**. The grid measures from the top-left corner and may leave an uneven gap at the right and bottom of the image. To center the grid, choose View > Rulers, and then drag the zero point to the center **B** of the image. (To find the center of the image, press Ctrl+T; a center point appears when Free Transform is in effect. Click the Cancel icon to turn off Free Transform.)

Make sure white is the foreground color, and then use the Rectangle tool to draw a shape covering the entire image. Photoshop Elements creates a new shape layer for it **C**. Now, click the Subtract From icon (or press the Alt key) and make sure Snap to Guides is selected. Draw a second rectangle inside the image **D**, aligned with the second grid line all the way around. Photoshop Elements removes the second rectangle from the first, leaving a nice new white border.

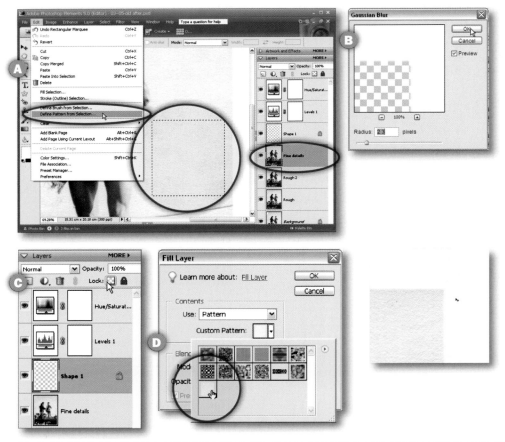

9. Age the Border.

To match the border with the image, we'll add a texture to it. Select the Fine Details layer in the Layers palette, and then use the Rectangular Marquee tool to select an area of the background with an even texture **A**. Choose Edit > Define Pattern from Selection, and name the selection "Photo Texture."

Zoom out to see the entire image. Next, blur the edge of the border to blend into the photo: Select the Shape layer, and choose Filter > Blur > Gaussian Blur **B**. Photoshop Elements prompts you to simplify the layer, which will turn it into pixels. Click OK. In the Gaussian Blur dialog box, set a radius of about 2 pixels.

Now we'll fill the edge with the new pattern. We only want to fill the edge, not the entire layer. Select the Shape layer, click the Lock **C** Transparent Pixels icon, and then choose Edit > Fill Layer. In the Fill Layer dialog box, choose the new pattern from the Custom Pattern Library. Reduce the opacity to 75%, and click OK **D**.

10. Add a Sepia Tone to the Image.

Let's give this whole photo a nostalgic look. Add a Hue/Saturation adjustment layer. Select Colorize, and then move the Hue slider to find a sepia tone you like. Change the saturation to make it richer or more muted. ▨

JAD

Performing Plastic Surgery

Remove those extra pounds electronically. You can warp, shift, pinch, and otherwise manipulate pixels with the Liquify filter.

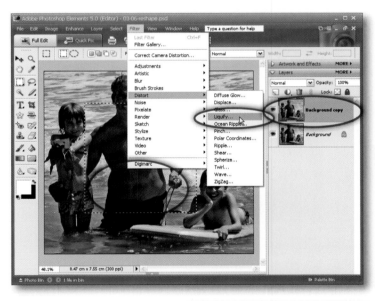

1. Open the Liquify Filter.

We'll retouch this image to help Jack remove those love handles. First, duplicate the layer to avoid permanently changing the original pixels; press Ctrl+Alt+J to duplicate the layer, and name it "Liquify." Select the area you want to work with, and then choose Filter > Distort > Liquify. The Liquify filter can run slowly if you apply it to an entire image, so it's more efficient to apply it to a selection.

INSIGHT

Liquify Tools. The Liquify filter manipulates areas of an image as if it were melting them. Each tool affects the pixels differently:

- **Warp** pushes pixels forward as you drag.
- **Turbulence** scrambles pixels to create fire, waves, and similar effects. To make the turbulence smoother, increase the Turbulent Jitter value in the Tool Options section.
- **Twirl Clockwise** rotates pixels clockwise as you drag.
- **Twirl Counterclockwise** rotates pixels counterclockwise as you drag.
- **Pucker** moves pixels toward the center of the brush area.
- **Bloat** moves pixels away from the center of the brush area.
- **Shift Pixels** moves pixels in a perpendicular direction from the stroke direction. Drag to move pixels to the left; Alt-drag to move them to the right.
- **Reflection** reflects the adjoining area. Drag down to reflect the area on the left of the brush, up to reflect the area to the right of the brush, right to reflect the area below the brush, and left to reflect the area above the brush.
- **Reconstruct** fully or partially reverses any changes you've made.

2. Shift Pixels.

There are several tools in the Liquify filter. For this job, we want to use the Shift Pixels tool. Zoom into the area you want to modify, and then drag the Shift Pixels tool along the side of the body **A**. To reduce the waistline, make one quick movement down the left side of the body, and then make one quick movement up the right side of the body. Use a smaller brush on the right side to avoid shifting the hand. You may also need to adjust the pixels in the water so that the shift isn't so obvious **B**.

3. Bulge the Muscles.

We can add muscles to Jack's upper arms using the Bloat tool. Select the tool and then click in the upper arm areas. This is an easy way to gain muscles without having to spend all that time in the gym. When you've got the arms the way you want them, click OK to apply the filter to the image. 🎞

Converting to Black and White

Transform a color photograph into a rich black-and-white image, adjusting the contrast and color channels to achieve the effect you want.

1. Duplicate the Layer.
To preserve the original pixels—and the original color data—we'll create a copy of the image to use in our conversion. Press Ctrl+J to duplicate the background layer. Name the layer Black and White.

> **T I P**
>
> **Partial Conversion.** For a dramatic effect, you can convert only part of an image, such as a background, to black and white. Select the area you want to convert, and then choose Enhance > Convert to Black and White. Only the selected area will be affected; the rest of the image remains in color.

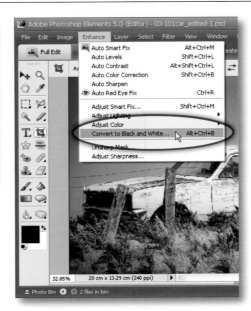

2. Convert to Black and White.
Choose Enhance > Convert to Black and White. The image immediately changes to black and white, but we're not done. We'll use the Convert to Black and White dialog box to make adjustments to the quality and character of the conversion.

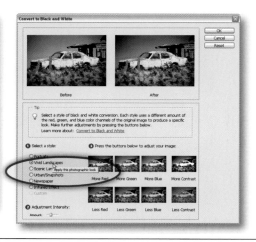

More Precision than Remove Color. You could convert an image to black and white using the Remove Color command, but the Convert to Black and White command gives you more control over the results. The Remove Color command removes the saturation, but leaves the image in RGB mode; it's equivalent to setting Saturation to –100 in the Hue/ Saturation dialog box.

3. Select a Style.

There are several style options. Experiment with each to see its effect on your image, and then select the one that comes closest to the look you want. The styles have been optimized for specific types of images, such as portraits or landscapes, but you can select any style for any image.

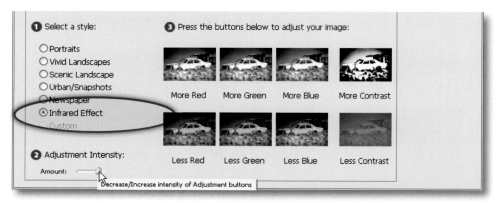

Using Black and White to Enrich Color. You can combine a black-and-white layer with a color layer for a richer, more nuanced image. Lower the opacity of the black-and-white layer to merge the two. Experiment with different blending modes for interesting effects.

4. Fine-tune the Conversion.

You can adjust the conversion settings by clicking the More or Less button to increase or decrease the contrast or the amount of data from each color channel included in the image. When you click a More or Less button, the style changes to Custom. Changes you make are reflected in the After thumbnail at the top of the dialog box.

To make your change more or less subtle, move the Intensity Adjustment slider before you click the More or Less button. Moving the slider to the right increases the effect of the change; moving it to the left provides a more subtle effect. The Intensity Adjustment slider affects future changes; it doesn't affect changes you've already made.

Click OK when you have the effect you want. Or, if you want to start over, click Reset. ▥

Replacing the Sky

Substitute the sky from another image to add drama to a photo.

1. Open Both Images.

In the world of digital imagery, you can mix and match images to create the scene you want. To substitute an element from one image for an element in another, first open both images in the Editor in Photoshop Elements.

2. Select the Sky.

With the main image active, select the Magic Wand tool. The Magic Wand tool recognizes color differences to make it easier to select irregular shapes. How the Magic Wand tool interprets color differences depends on the Tolerance setting in the Options bar. To select this sky, we'll get the best results with a tolerance of about 40%. Deselect Contiguous because the bits of sky are not all next to each other; some are amid the trees, for example. Click in the sky to make the initial selection.

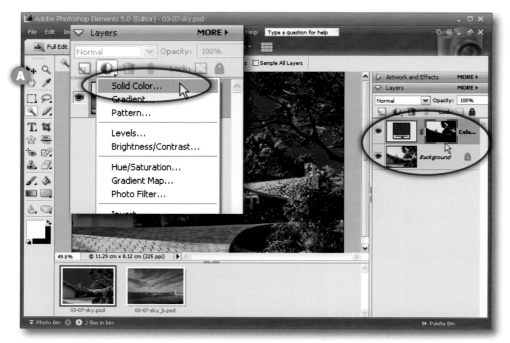

3. Refine the Selection.

The Magic Wand tool has picked up areas that aren't actually part of the sky, including highlights in the chimney and the cobblestone. To remove those from the selection, create a Solid Color adjustment layer **A**. Choose a bright color from the color picker, such as a bright blue. Click OK. Photoshop Elements fills the selection area with the bright color. Now, to see just the mask, Alt-click the layer mask thumbnail in the Layers palette. Use the Paintbrush tool to paint out the bits of white in the house, chimney, and driveway **B**. Click the solid color thumbnail to display the full image again to see what you've missed; the selected areas show up clearly with the bright blue color. You can also paint the mask while you're viewing the entire image **C**.

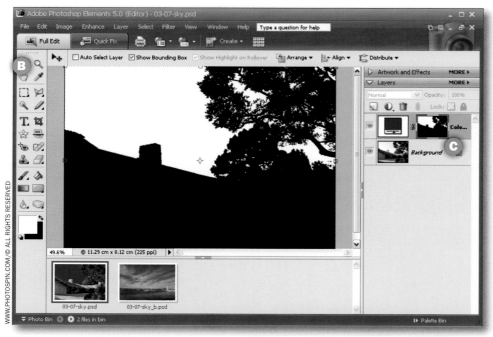

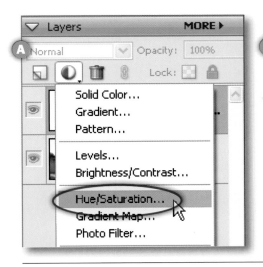

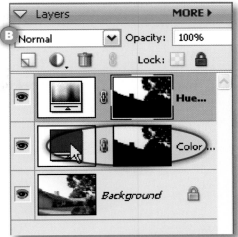

4. Create a Hue/Saturation Adjustment Layer.

When nothing but sky remains in the bright color, Control-Click the layer mask thumbnail in the Layers palette to select the sky. Then, create a Hue/Saturation adjustment layer **A**. We're not actually going to make any changes in this adjustment layer, so just click OK. The same layer mask thumbnail appears in the Hue/Saturation adjustment layer. Delete the Solid Color adjustment layer **B**.

5. Merge the Images.

Now we're ready to bring in the sky from the other image. Click the Photo bin icon in the lower-left corner of the Editor to display both images **C**. Then drag the background layer of the image with the new sky onto the first image. Photoshop Elements adds a new layer to the original image. Name the new layer "Sky." Position the sky however you want it.

Now, Alt-click on the dividing line between the Hue/Saturation adjustment layer and the Sky layer to group the two layers **D**. To match this new sky just a bit better with the original image, reduce the opacity to 75%. 🖩

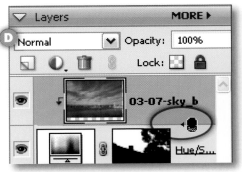

Removing a Person

Unclutter your image by removing extra people, animals, or objects using the Healing Brush tool.

TIP

Ghosting. If you want someone's presence to become a bit more ethereal, use the Healing Brush tool to remove them, and then apply an opacity of 25% or so to bring back a hint of their existence.

1. Duplicate the Layer.

Before you do anything else, press Ctrl+Alt+J to duplicate the layer. Name it "Remove."

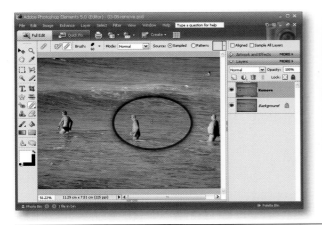

2. Paint Out Extras.

Select the Healing Brush tool. Select Aligned, and choose a larger brush size. Then, click a source point and simply paint over the person, animal, or object you want to remove from the photo. Photoshop Elements "heals" the area by analyzing the surrounding colors and filling in the background appropriately.

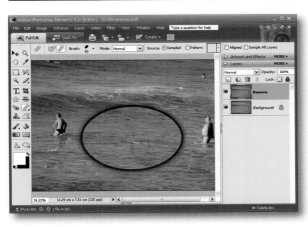

3. Touch up the Area.

To make the change less obvious, you may need to touch up the area around the missing person or object a little bit. Remember that you can always press Ctrl+Z to undo and start over. ⊞

4

PHOTO ENHANCING

Adding That Extra Sizzle to Your Digital Photography Adventures

YOU'VE PICKED UP THE BASICS, and you're getting more comfortable with the tools in Photoshop Elements. Now you're ready for the more advanced world of photo enhancement. In Chapter 4, we'll show you how to mix blending modes and filters with a real creative flair.

Blending In

Layers, layers, and more layers—the best Photoshop Elements projects rely on how layers interact with each other. Blending modes make all the difference, as they determine how much you can see of a layer that lies beneath another, and how the colors on those two layers interact. And once you understand how blending modes work with neutral colors (white, black, or neutral gray, depending on the blending mode), you can get even more creative with filters. You can get great, interesting results with blending modes. Experiment!

Storytelling

A photograph captures a moment in time. Sometimes, having the action stop for a brief second can be quite poignant. Other times, though, the mood of the occasion is sacrificed. With the help of Photoshop Elements, we can reintroduce the drama of a scene. For example, we'll show you how to add movement with a motion blur and then blend that movement convincingly into the image with the use of adjustment layers and layer masks. Motion blur restores the excitement of rushing water that was present when the photograph was taken.

Close Shave

Sure, you could ask your subject to use a razor before you take his photo, but if you're capturing a spontaneous moment, that's not a great option. One of the cooler ways to use the Dust & Scratches filter is to shave a subject's face—digitally. Or use the Reduce Noise filter to smooth out a complexion. There are so many great filters in Photoshop Elements that you can look quite shabby in real life and still clean up very well in a final photo. We'll help you keep your friends and family looking spiffy.

pop Pop POP

Why settle for good when you can make a photo great? We'll take a perfectly fine photograph, nicely in focus, and improve it dramatically using Jack Davis's "Make it look better" technique. Jack is kind enough to share this trick, which uses an intriguing combination of filters and layers to make your images appear to pop off the page. When people ask how you got such great results, go ahead and tell them you're just a very skilled photographer who captured the image at the right moment. We'll keep your secret.

Understanding Blending Modes

How layers interact with each other in Photoshop Elements depends on the blending mode you assign. You can apply blending modes to layers in the Layers palette or to brushes in the Options bar. Most blending modes have a neutral color, a color that results in no effect. Blending modes are grouped in the menu according to their neutral colors and the type of effect they have.

Normal Modes

There is no neutral color for the Normal or Dissolve blending modes.

Normal, the default, hides pixels beneath the top layer unless the top layer is partially or fully transparent. When the layer is not opaque, it transitions to transparency smoothly.

Dissolve is similar to Normal, but it transitions to transparency in a speckled pattern. This blending mode randomly replaces pixels with the color of either the top layer or the layer beneath it, so that the top layer appears to dissolve into the layers beneath it.

Darkening Modes

When you use any of the blending modes in this group, the resulting color is always darker than the original. Their neutral color is white.

Darken replaces pixels in the underlying layers with those in the top layer whenever the pixels in the top layer are darker.

Multiply multiplies the color in the underlying layers with the color in the top layer.

Color Burn darkens the color in the underlying layers to reflect the color in the top layer by increasing the contrast.

Linear Burn darkens the color in the underlying layers to reflect the color in the top layer by decreasing the brightness.

Lightening Modes

When you use any of the blending modes in this group, the resulting color is always lighter than the original. Their neutral color is black.

Lighten replaces pixels in the underlying layers with those in the top layer wherever the pixels in the top layer are lighter.

Screen multiplies the inverse of the colors in the underlying and top layers. The effect is similar to projecting multiple slides on top of each other.

Color Dodge brightens the underlying colors to reflect the color in the top layer by decreasing the contrast.

Linear Dodge brightens the underlying colors to reflect the color in the top layer by increasing the brightness.

Overlay Modes

Blending modes in this group all result in greater contrast. Their neutral color is 50% gray.

Overlay either multiplies or screens the colors, depending on the colors in the underlying layers. Patterns or colors overlay the existing pixels while preserving the highlights and shadows of the underlying layers.

Soft Light darkens or lightens the colors. The colors in the top layer act as a diffused spotlight shining on the image.

Hard Light multiplies or screens the colors. The colors in the top layer act as a harsh spotlight shining on the image.

Vivid Light burns or dodges the colors by increasing or decreasing the contrast. If the color in the top layer (which is used as the light source) is lighter than 50% gray, the image is lightened by decreasing the contrast. If the color in the top layer is darker than 50% gray, the image is darkened by increasing the contrast.

Linear Light burns or dodges the colors by increasing or decreasing the brightness. If the color in the top layer (which is used as the light source) is lighter than 50% gray, the image is lightened by increasing the brightness. If the color in the top layer is darker than 50% gray, the image is darkened by decreasing the brightness.

Pin Light replaces the colors, depending on the color in the top layer. If the color in the top layer (acting as the light source) is lighter than 50% gray, pixels darker than that color are replaced. If the color in the top layer is darker than 50% gray, pixels lighter than that color are replaced.

Hard Mix reduces colors to white, black, red, green, blue, yellow, cyan, and magenta, depending on the colors in the top and underlying layers.

Difference Modes

The blending modes in this group are based on the differences between the colors in the top layer and the underlying layers. Their neutral color is black.

Difference compares the colors in the top layer with those in the underlying layers, and it subtracts the darker colors from the lighter ones.

Exclusion creates an effect similar to Difference mode, but results in lower contrast.

Hue Modes

The blending modes in this group affect the color values of the image. These modes have no neutral color.

Hue replaces the hue of the underlying layers with that of the top layer, but doesn't change the luminance and saturation values of the underlying layers.

Saturation replaces the saturation of the underlying layers with that of the top layer.

Color replaces both the hue and the saturation of the underlying layers with those of the top layer. This blending mode preserves the gray levels in the image. It's a great mode to use to colorize monochrome images and to tint color images.

Luminosity replaces only the luminance of the underlying colors with that of the top layer. ▥

Dodging and Burning

Use blending modes to dodge and burn, or lighten and darken, images.

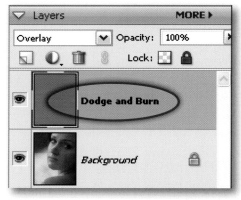

1. Create a New Layer.

We'll use a blending mode to lighten the face in this photograph. First, press Ctrl+Shift+N to create a new layer. In the New Layer dialog box, choose Overlay from the Mode menu, and select Fill with Overlay-Neutral Color (50% Gray). Name the layer "Dodge and burn."

Photoshop Elements creates a 50% gray layer, but because the Overlay mode has a neutral color of 50% gray, the layer has no effect on the image.

2. Paint to Lighten Areas.

When we're working with the Overlay mode, anything in the new layer that is lighter than 50% gray lightens the image beneath, and anything that is darker than 50% gray darkens the image. To lighten, or dodge, the image, we'll paint with white. Set white as the foreground color in the toolbox. Then, select the Paintbrush tool and set the opacity to 10%. For best results, use a soft brush. Paint everywhere you want to lighten the image. In this photo, we'll lighten the face a bit, especially around the lower portion of the eye. We like to think of this as painting with light.

3. Paint to Darken Areas.

You can use the same technique to darken areas of the image. Change the foreground color to black, and use the same paintbrush. Paint over areas you want to darken, or burn. The layer thumbnail in the Layers palette shows where you've painted light areas and dark areas.

4. Add Noise.

Let's add a bit of noise to this image to approximate the grain of a printed photograph. Press Ctrl+Shift+N to create another layer. Choose Overlay from the Mode menu again, and select Fill with Overlay-Neutral Color (50% Gray). Name the layer "Noise." With the Noise layer selected, choose Filter > Noise > Add Noise. Select Monochromatic in the Add Noise dialog box to ensure that you don't change the colors in the image. Set the amount to about 5% for good results with this image. The grain is applied to the Noise layer, but it affects all the layers beneath.

The grain is nice, but it will look better if we smooth it out a bit. With the Noise layer selected, choose Filter > Blur > Gaussian Blur, and set the blur to 1 pixel.

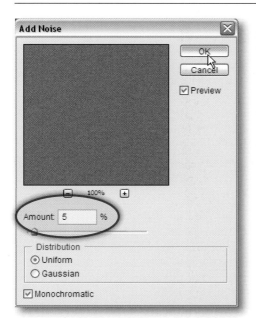

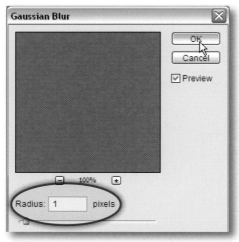

Adding Motion Blur

Emphasize—or create—movement in a specific part of an image using the Motion Blur filter.

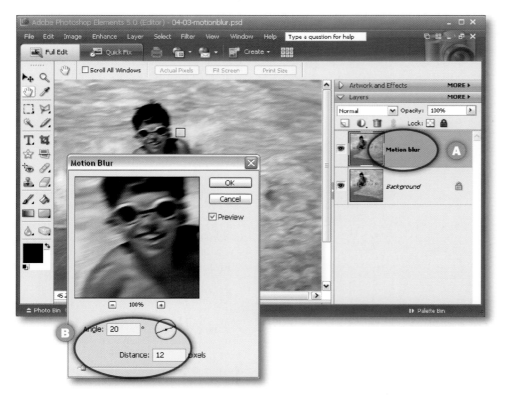

1. Apply the Motion Blur Filter.

We'll emphasize the motion of the waves in this photo. You can use motion blur to indicate movement of a vehicle, an animal, a bouncing ball, or just about any other part of an image. As with so many of our projects, we'll start by duplicating the background layer **A**. Press Ctrl+Alt+J, and name the layer "Motion blur."

With the Motion Blur layer selected, choose Filter > Blur > Motion Blur **B**.

In the Motion Blur dialog box, set a distance and an angle. The distance determines the amount of blur, and the angle determines the direction of the motion. For the waves, we'll use a distance of 12 pixels and an angle that matches the direction of the water, about 20 degrees. Click OK to apply the filter.

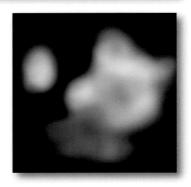

2. Apply the Motion Blur Selectively.

We've applied the Motion Blur filter to the entire image. In some cases, that might be desirable, but in this image, the child should be still as the water moves. In order to choose where the motion blur will be applied, we'll need to create a mask. To create a mask, we need to create an adjustment layer between the first two layers. Select the background layer, and then click the Create Adjustment Layer, and choose Levels **A**. We don't actually want to make any changes to the levels, so just click OK to close the dialog box.

We want the mask to affect the Motion blur layer, so press the Alt key and click between the adjustment layer and the Motion blur layer to create a clipping group **B**. An arrow appears on the Motion blur layer in the Layers palette. Now, fill the mask with black to hide the blur entirely: Set black as the foreground color in the Toolbox, select the layer mask thumbnail in the Layers palette, and press Alt+Backspace. Now the mask is black and the blur does not affect the image at all.

Set white as the foreground color. Select the Paintbrush tool, with an opacity of about 25%. Paint wherever you want the motion blur to show. To hide the motion blur from an area, paint with black.

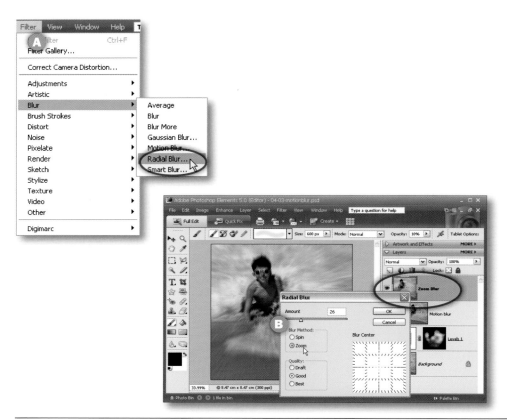

3. Add a Zoom Blur.

To focus the motion of the water around the child, we'll add a zoom blur. Once again, duplicate the background layer: select the background layer, and press Ctrl+Alt+J; name the layer "Zoom Blur." Move the Zoom Blur layer to the top of the Layers palette.

Choose Filter > Blur > Radial Blur **A**. Select Zoom in the Radial Blur dialog box. The Zoom setting blurs along radial lines, as if you were zooming in or out of the image. Unfortunately, there is no preview option in this filter, so you have to make your best guess. By default, the zoom focus is centered in the image. In the grid, called the Blur Center Box, move the origin of the blur to roughly align it to the area where you want to focus the zoom **B**. For this image, we'll move it to the upper-left quarter, because that's where the child is. Select Best for Quality, and we'll select about 26 for Amount. Click OK and cross your fingers that it's in the right spot.

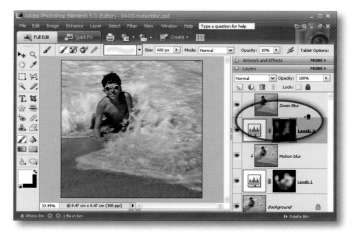

4. Apply the Zoom Blur Selectively.

As with the motion blur, we've applied the zoom blur to the entire image. To apply the blur selectively, we'll use another mask. As before, create a Levels adjustment layer, but make no changes to the levels. Move the adjustment layer below the Zoom Blur layer. Press Alt while you click between the two layers to group them. Select black as the foreground color, and then select the layer mask thumbnail, and press Alt+Backspace. Paint with white as the foreground color wherever you want the zoom blur effect. The motion blur paired with the zoom blur gives a much more realistic wave.

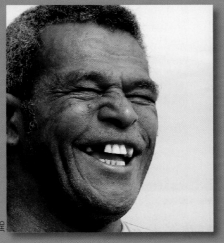

Shaving Digitally

You don't need a razor to remove stubble in Photoshop Elements. The Dust & Scratches filter does the trick.

1. Apply the Dust & Scratches Filter.

The Dust & Scratches filter was designed to repair physical damage in photos, but the filter works just as well to remove specks in the picture itself. To remove unwanted stubble, first duplicate the background layer **A** (Ctrl+Alt+J) and name it "Dust and Scratches."

In the Dust & Scratches dialog box, set the Radius and Threshold values **B**. The Radius determines the size of the detail to remove. For the stubble in this image, 2 pixels is about right. The Threshold lets you reintroduce some of the fine detail and texture after the stubble has been removed. Choose 30 levels for this image. Watch the preview window as you adjust the Radius and Threshold; zoom in to see how the settings affect the chin. Hold the mouse button down over the preview window **C** to see what the image looked like before you made any changes. When you're satisfied that you've removed the stubble, click OK.

2. Create a Mask.

The Dust & Scratches filter applies to the entire image, so this gentleman's eyelashes, eyebrows, and other areas are affected. We really only want to remove the stubble, so once again, we'll need a mask to help us apply the filter selectively.

Create any kind of adjustment layer, but don't make any adjustments; just click OK. Then, select the layer mask thumbnail in the Layers palette. Select black as the foreground color in the toolbox, and press Alt+Backspace to fill the mask with black. To group the mask layer with the Dust & Scratches layer, press the Alt key as you click between the layers.

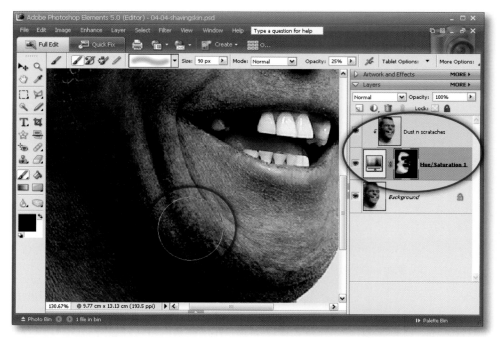

3. Shave.

Remember, where the mask is black, the layer above is hidden, and where it's white, the layer is revealed. Set the foreground color to white. Select the Paintbrush tool and choose a brush size. A large brush with soft edges usually works best for this task. Reduce the opacity for a subtler effect. Then select the layer mask thumbnail, and paint over the stubble to give your subject a cleaner shave.

You can use the same brush to reduce the wrinkles and fine lines around the eyes. As you work, the layer mask thumbnail reflects where you've painted. Move back and forth between black and white to remove the detail and restore it. Alt-click the mask to see it without the image beneath it; this can be useful to help you smooth out areas that aren't evenly painted.

Smoothing Complexions

Remember the smile, not the blemishes. You can overcome skin flaws with the Reduce Noise filter.

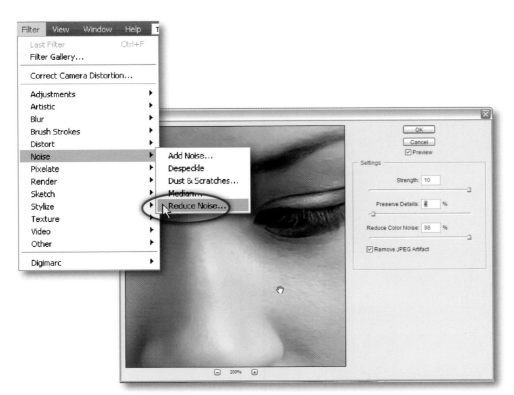

1. Apply the Reduce Noise Filter.

Subtle skin blemishes are a sort of noise, a distraction from the beauty of your subject. So it's only appropriate that we'll use the Reduce Noise filter to soften those distractions. Start by duplicating the background layer (Ctrl+Alt+J), and name the new layer "Reduce Noise." Then choose Filter > Noise > Reduce Noise.

Zoom in to see the areas you want to smooth. Increase the Strength to a high value and keep the Preserve Detail value low. In this case, we want to lose the detail, and the lower Preserve Detail setting gives us smoother results. Select a high value for Reduce Color Noise; this is especially helpful if the skin is mottled or reddish. Select Remove JPEG Artifact; even if you don't see any, this setting won't hurt anything. Click OK to apply the filter.

2. Create a Mask for the Filter.

We've applied the Reduce Noise filter to the entire image, but we really only want to apply it to specific areas. So, we'll use a mask. Create an adjustment layer—any kind of adjustment layer will do—and click OK in its dialog box without changing any settings. Then set the foreground color to black, select the layer mask thumbnail, and press Alt+Backspace to fill the mask with black. Group the mask layer with the Reduce Noise layer by pressing Alt and clicking the line between the two layers.

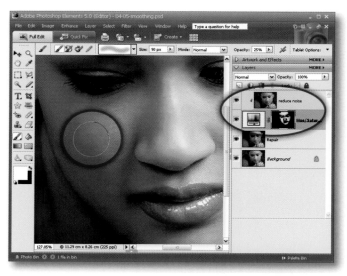

3. Paint on the Mask.

While the entire mask is black, the filter has no effect on the image. Set the foreground color to white. Select the Paintbrush tool, and reduce its opacity. Then, paint wherever you want the Reduce Noise layer to show. You may want to increase the opacity and the brush size in some areas of the image. 🖮

T I P

Foreground and Background.
To quickly set the foreground to white and the background to black, press D (for default) on the keyboard. To switch the foreground and background colors, press X.

Enhancing Contrast

Add a bit of pizzazz to an image by enhancing the natural contrast within it.

1. Create a New Layer.

We'll make the contrast in our image more striking using blending modes and blur effects. First, duplicate the background layer (Ctrl+Alt+J) and name the new layer "Blur." Select Soft Light from the Mode menu in the New Layer dialog box. Already, the contrast is much more apparent in the image.

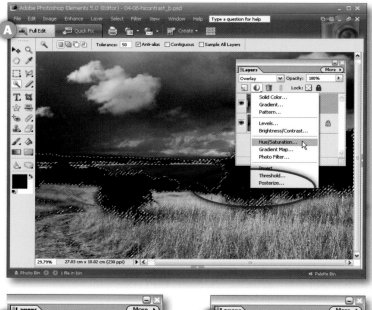

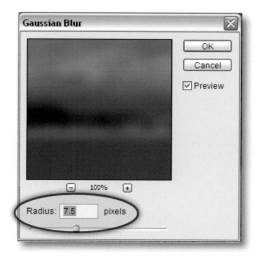

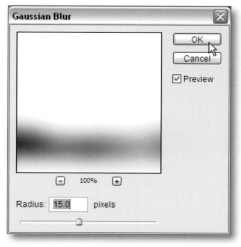

2. Create a Mask.

The blending mode applies to the entire layer. While we've gained lovely contrast in part of the image, we've lost detail in the shadows. We'll need a mask to select which portions of the image the blending mode affects. Select the Magic Wand **A** tool, and set its Tolerance to about 50; deselect Contiguous. Click in a dark area of the image to select all the dark areas.

Now, create an adjustment layer, and click OK without changing any settings in its dialog box. The selection appears in the layer mask thumbnail. However, we need its inverse. Select the layer mask thumbnail and press Ctrl+I to invert it **B**. Move the adjustment layer beneath the Blur layer. Press the Alt key, and click the line between the adjustment layer **C** and the Blur layer to group them.

3. Add a Blur Effect.

The blending mode is only affecting the areas where we want to show contrast, but its edges are a bit harsh. A Gaussian blur will soften the effect and provide a slight glow. Select the Blur layer, and choose Filter > Blur > Gaussian Blur. Set the blur to about 7 pixels, and click OK.

Now, apply the same effect to the mask itself. Select the layer mask thumbnail, choose Filter > Blur > Gaussian Blur, and click OK. The image blends together more smoothly. To smooth it even more, select the Paintbrush tool, set it to a low opacity, and paint out the mask to darken some areas. 🛅

Enhancing Detail

Transform a good photograph into an eye-popping image by enhancing the detail and edges in the photo.

1. Duplicate the Background Layer.

We'll pull out the edges in this image, but we don't want to alter the original pixels. So start by duplicating the image (Ctrl+Alt+J). Name the duplicate "High Pass."

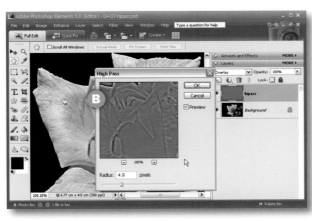

2. Apply the High Pass Filter.

The High Pass filter plucks out the edge details where there are sharp color transitions and suppresses the rest of the image. The results can look a little strange, as you'll see in the High Pass dialog box, which opens with default settings applied. Drag the Radius slider all the way to the left to start from scratch. The preview image turns 50% gray **A**. As you drag the slider to the right, the edges and detail of the image appear **B**. Typically, 4–5 pixels gives the results we want. Click OK to apply the filter.

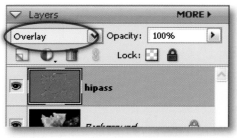

3. Reveal the Image.

All we're seeing is the filter effect, not the image beneath it. To see both, we need to use a blending mode with a neutral color of 50% gray. Select the High Pass layer, and then choose Overlay from the Mode menu in the Layers palette. The gray disappears, and the image is sharper and more intense than it was originally.

> **T I P**
>
> **Preview As You Work.** We applied the filter first and then applied the blending mode. If you want to see the image itself as you adjust the filter settings, apply the Overlay blending mode when you duplicate the layer.

4. Selectively Apply the Filter.

The filter applies to the entire layer, but you may want to apply it to only a particular part of the image. As you might guess, you'll need a layer mask to do that. Create an adjustment layer, and click OK to close its dialog box without making any changes. Set black as the foreground layer, select the layer mask thumbnail, and press Alt+Backspace to fill the mask with black **A**. Press Alt and click between the adjustment layer and the Blur layer to group them.

Then, set the foreground color to white, and paint over the areas you want to sharpen **B**. For the best results, reduce the opacity of the brush. ▥

Using How to Wow Presets. The CD included with this book contains all kinds of goodies, including custom shapes and layer styles. To use these in Photoshop Elements, you need to first copy them to your hard drive. We've included shortcuts to help you copy them to the right folders.

On the How to Wow CD, right-click the How to Wow Shapes folder, and choose Copy. Then, double-click the Shortcut to Shapes folder to open the appropriate folder on your hard disk. Right-click in the folder and choose Paste. Next, right-click the How to Wow Styles folder, and choose Copy. Double-click the Shortcut to Styles folder, right-click in the folder, and choose Paste. You'll need to restart Photoshop Elements to make the new presets active.

If you need to get to the folders on your own, you'll find styles in Documents and Settings\ All Users\ Application Data\ Adobe\ Photoshop Elements\ 5.0\ Photo Creations\ Special Effects\ Layer Styles, and shapes are in Documents and Settings\ All Users\ Application Data\ Adobe\ Photoshop Elements\ 5.0\ Photo Creations\.

For more on working with the How to Wow presets, see the "Read Me" file on the top level of this book's companion CD.

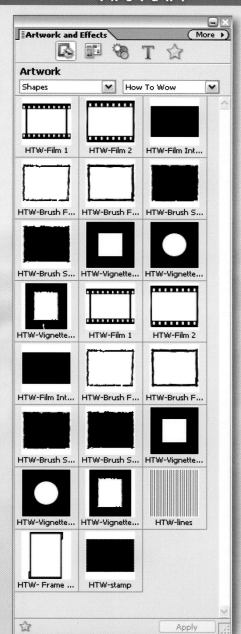

5

CREATIVE PROJECTS

*Adding the WOW Factor
to Your Projects and
Getting the Results That
Will Impress*

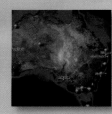

IT'S TIME TO GET CREATIVE. Obviously, the best fun can be had when there are no rules. We'll get your creative juices flowing by transforming photos into watercolors, adding tattoos where none exist in real life, enhancing a book cover, creating a card to easily show off your photos, and more.

The lessons in this chapter merely serve as a starting point. We know you have a Salvador Dali or Andy Warhol lurking beneath the surface. It's time to let your creative genius come out to play.

Pen and Ink

Don't bother putting on an art smock, and you won't have to clean up your supplies. But you will create an exciting and realistic-looking watercolor with pen-and-ink line work. Choosing the right image to work with is critical to the effect; landscape shots work very well. Let us show you how to become one of the great masters of watercolor—without any spills.

That's a Wrap

You needn't spend money on commercial wrapping paper when you can create more meaningful, personalized paper with Photoshop Elements. We'll create a customized pattern to repeat across any paper size. Custom paper that includes the recipient's name or a special message is especially nice for birthdays, anniversaries, and graduations, but you can also make your own holiday paper or create a tasteful all-purpose design. To get a head start, take advantage of the presets that are included on the How to Wow CD.

A Present of Presets

Our special gift to you is the gift of presets on the How to Wow CD, including brushes, custom shapes, layer styles, and more. We use some of the How to Wow presets in the projects in this book, but you can use all of them for your own projects.

Sign On the Dotted Line

All the great works of art include the artists' signatures. Carry on the tradition by signing your works of art in Photoshop Elements. Scan in a signature, and then we'll walk you through the steps to create a custom brush from it so that, with a simple click, you can lay claim to your work. As a bonus, you can use the signature to create a tasteful, subtle watermark to protect your work online.

Making an Instant Watercolor

Transform a photograph into a pen-and-ink watercolor painting using the Smart Blur filter.

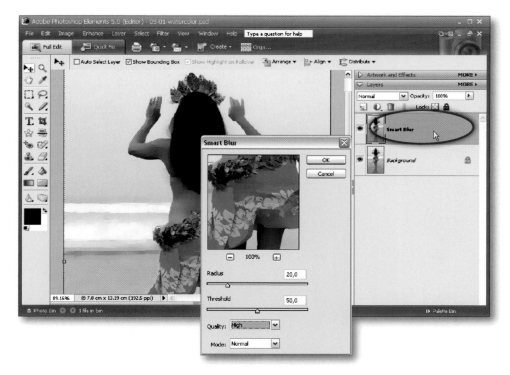

1. Create the Watercolor Effect.

Some photographs almost call out for a watercolor effect. We'll use this image of a hula dancer, ideal because of its bright colors and simple background. First, press Ctrl+Alt+J to duplicate the background layer; name the new layer "Smart Blur." Select the Smart Blur layer, and choose Filter > Blur > Smart Blur.

The Smart Blur filter blurs an image where pixels that differ meet, based on the settings in the Smart Blur dialog box. The Radius setting determines how far the filter searches for dissimilar pixels to blur. The Threshold setting determines how different the pixels' values must be. Experiment with the Radius and Threshold sliders to get the effect you want. It's usually best to choose High for the Quality. Leave the Mode set to Normal in this step. Click OK.

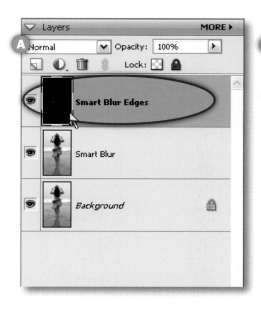

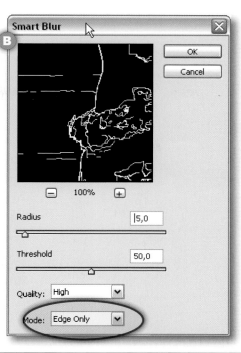

2. Trace the Edges.

To give our watercolor painting a little more definition, we'll add pen-and-ink edges. And we'll use the same Smart Blur filter to do it. Duplicate the background layer again **A** (Ctrl+Alt+J), and name the new layer Smart Blur Edges. Drag the new layer above the "Smart Blur" layer in the Layers palette. Now, choose Filter > Blur > Smart Blur. This time, we'll choose Edge Only from the Mode menu **B**. The filter traces the edges in the image. You can increase the Threshold setting to see fewer lines. Click OK when you're satisfied.

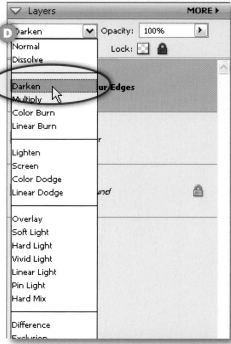

3. Add the Edges to the Watercolor Image.

At this point, all we see are the edges, and they're in white. We want the edges to be black, so let's invert the layer **C**. Select the Smart Blur Edges layer and press Ctrl+I. Presto. The edges are black. We still see only the edges, but we want to see the watercolor layer as well. We'll turn to our old friends, blending modes, to make that happen. Because the background of the Smart Blur Edges layer is white, we'll want a blending mode that has white for its neutral color. Apply the Darken blending mode **D** to see nice black outlines surrounding the colored areas.

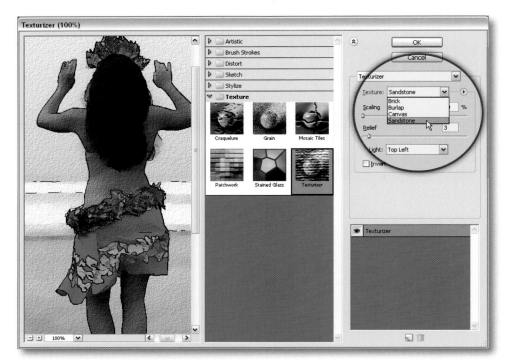

4. Add a Canvas Texture.

Of course, a watercolor is usually painted on a canvas of some kind, so we'll add a subtle texture to the image. First, create a new layer that is a composite of all the visible layers: press Ctrl+Alt+Shift+E. Name the layer "Texture."

With the Texture layer selected, choose Filter > Texture > Texturizer. The Texturizer filter adds texture to an image. There are several options in the Texturizer dialog box. Change the settings on the right. From the Texture menu, choose Sandstone. The Scaling slider determines how coarse the texture is, and the Relief slider determines how deep the texture appears to be. You can also change the lighting or invert the texture. Experiment with all the settings to find the one you like. Click OK and take a look at your masterpiece! ▥

Creating Painless Tattoos

If you're not ready to etch a tattoo into your skin, use blending modes and warping features to add tattoos digitally.

1. Create the Text Layer.

What better way to send a message than to express it in a tattoo? We'll add "I Love how to wow" to this woman's arm, but you could send birthday greetings, congratulations, or a sign of your devotion using the same method. We'll start by creating a text layer.

Select the Horizontal Type tool. Click on the page and type your tattoo message. Photoshop Elements automatically creates a new layer for the text. Select the text, and then apply a font and type size from the Options bar. We'll use a script font for a typical tattoo look. You can also change the leading, or line spacing, in the Options bar. To reposition the text block, move the cursor off to the side until it becomes a pointer, and then move the text.

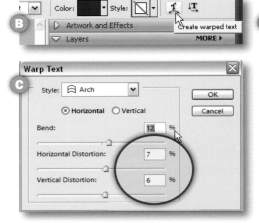

2. Curve the Tattoo Around the Arm.

Our tattoo is never going to look real if it doesn't curve where the arm curves, so we'll warp it. Select the text with the Type tool **A**. Then click the Create Warped Text icon **B**. In the Warp Text dialog box **C**, select the style, bend, and distortions. We'll use the Arch style for this arm, and a Bend value of about 12. Adjust the values slowly to match the arm in the image. We'll use a Horizontal Distortion value of +7 and a Vertical Distortion value of +6 because the front of the arm is slightly closer to us.

Don't panic if you don't get it just right the first time. It's easy to tweak the warp effect. Just select the text and click the Create Warped Text icon again. Then adjust the settings.

3. Adjust the Color.

You can choose any ink color you want. Blue is common in tattoos, so that's what we'll go with here. Select the text again. Then, select a color from the Color menu in the Options bar **A**. The color's a bit bright. To make this text really seem to be part of the skin, we'll need to use a blending mode. Select Multiply for the Mode for the layer **B**, and then change the opacity to about 60%.

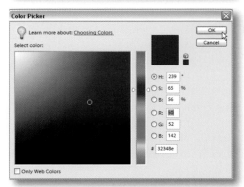

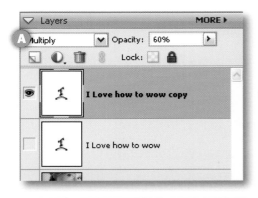

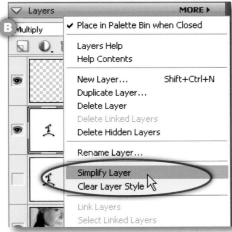

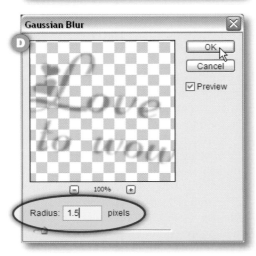

4. Blur the Tattoo.

To make this tattoo look more realistic, we'll need to blur its edges a bit. When you blur text, you can no longer edit it, so let's duplicate the text layer first. That way, if we need to make changes later, we can. Press Ctrl+Alt+J to duplicate the layer **A**; name the new layer "Blur." With the Blur layer selected, choose Simplify Layer from the More menu in the Layers palette **B**. The Simplify Layer command builds text from pixels, rather than a vector font.

Now that the text is in pixels, we can apply a blur filter. Choose Filter > Blur > Gaussian Blur **C**. Roughly 1.5 pixels gives a realistic look for this image **D**, but you may need a different setting for other images. ▥

T I P

Zoom, Zoom, Zoom. To zoom in quickly, press Ctrl+ on the keyboard. To zoom out quickly, press Ctrl- on the keyboard. Press the spacebar to use the Hand tool to pan across an image.

Creating Custom Wrapping Paper

Create personalized wrapping paper to cover special gifts. You can use custom patterns in any Photoshop Elements project.

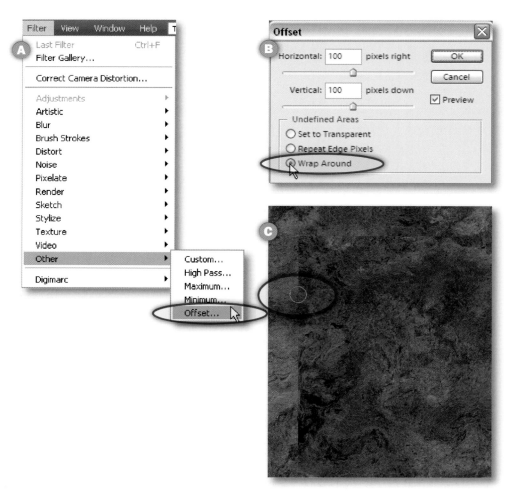

1. Prepare the Background Texture.

Make the wrapping paper as meaningful as the gift. Start by creating a background texture. You can create a texture using filters in Photoshop Elements, or, as we've done here, scan one in. It's a lovely texture, but when the pattern repeats, we'll see where the edges join. To ensure the pattern repeats seamlessly, we'll use the Healing Brush tool.

We have a white background layer, with the texture layer on top of it. Select the texture layer, and then choose Filter > Other > Offset **A**. Now move the Vertical and Horizontal sliders so that the edges are 100 pixels right and 100 pixels down and select Wrap Around **B**. Click OK, and then select the Healing Brush tool. Use an elliptical brush with spacing of about 37%. Alt-click to select a source point and brush over the edge **C**. Select different source points to keep from repeating patterns. You can also use the Healing Brush tool to pull shading into other areas, creating more continuity in your pattern.

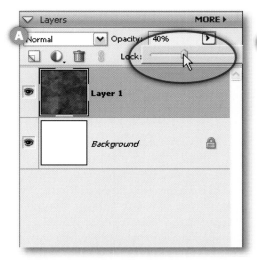

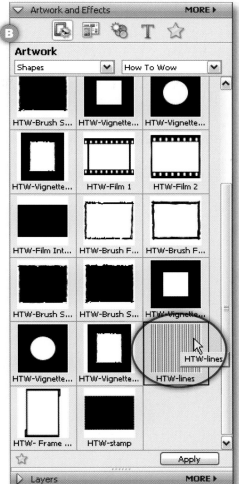

2. Add Graphics to the Pattern.

So that shapes will show up against your background, reduce the opacity of the texture layer **A**. Now, select the Artwork and Effects Panel. Choose a shape from the artwork menu and select How to Wow. We'll choose Lines, a shape from the How to Wow CD **B**. Click and drag over the texture **C**. Photoshop Elements automatically creates a new layer for the shape; rename the layer "Lines." So that this pattern repeats seamlessly, make sure there's enough space on the edges to distribute the lines evenly. An easy way to do this is to position the lines at the top-left corner of the page, and then press Ctrl+T for the Free Transform tool. Drag the pattern in from the right to match the edge. Let's reduce the opacity of this layer to about 15% to give a light striped texture.

Add other shapes, as you like **D**. We used butterflies and leaves. You can rotate shapes, change their color, and change their opacity. Each time you create a shape, Photoshop Elements creates a new layer for it, so it's easy to reposition them.

3. Add a Message.

We're making wrapping paper for a birthday present, so we want to personalize it for the birthday girl. You could add "Happy Anniversary," "Merry Christmas," or any other message you like. Use the Horizontal Type tool to create the text. Photoshop Elements creates a separate layer for it. Select the font and color from the Options bar.

The text should repeat in a single line across the page, so it needs to fill the pattern. You can make it fill the area by increasing the type size or by dragging the text field to expand it. Finally, let's change the opacity of the text to 70% to blend it in with the design.

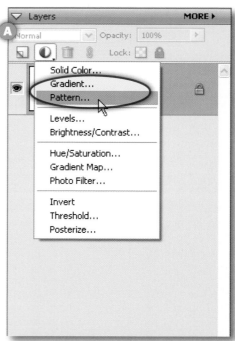

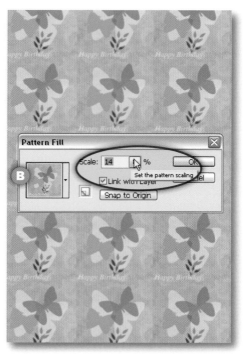

4. Repeat the Pattern.

When you have the pattern the way you want it, save it as a pattern you can reuse in Photoshop Elements. Press Ctrl+A to select everything in the document, and then choose Edit > Define Pattern From Selection **A**. Give it a name you'll recognize later.

To use the pattern, create a new Photoshop Elements document the size of the wrapping paper you want to create. Then, select the Create Adjustment Layer icon in the Layers palette, and choose Pattern. Select the pattern you just created. Then use the slider in the Pattern Fill dialog box **B** to scale the pattern across the page. Click OK when you're satisfied. Finally, print the paper and wrap your present!

Adding a Digital Signature

Sign your creative projects with a brush made from your own signature.

1. Scan In the Signature.

It's difficult to sign your name with a mouse. Instead, sign your name on paper with a big, bold pen, and then scan it in. Choose File > Get Photos > From Scanner in the Organizer. Your scanning options depend on the scanner you use, but make sure you scan in grayscale and at a resolution of at least 300 dpi. If you're scanning a small signature, use 600 dpi. When the signature is in the Organizer, select it and choose Edit > Go To Standard Edit.

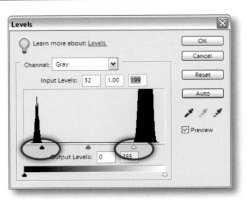

2. Clean Up the Signature.

Texture from the pen and from the original paper is usually included in the scanned image, especially if the paper is off-white. Select the Create Adjustment Layer icon in the Layers palette, and then choose Levels. In the Levels dialog box, drag the white point slider further left than the detail in the histogram, and move the black point slider further to the right than the black spike in the histogram. This will give you a clean black-and-white signature.

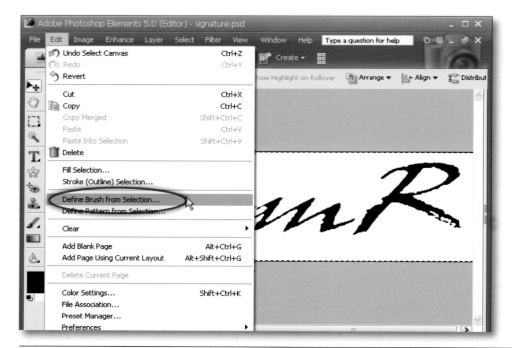

3. Create a Signature Brush.

You can create your own brushes in Photoshop Elements, which you can then use in any project. To create a brush from your signature, press Ctrl+A to select everything, and then choose Edit > Define Brush From Selection. You can give the brush your name, or name it "Signature."

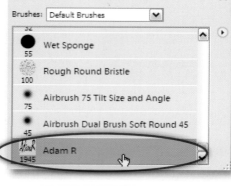

4. Paint On the Signature.

Open a Photoshop Elements project. We'll use the watercolor project we created earlier in this chapter. Create a new layer for the signature. Then, select the Paintbrush tool. Select the paintbrush you created from the list of brushes available. By default, it's probably quite large. Resize the brush as appropriate for your project. Select a color for the signature. We like to use the Eyedropper tool to sample a color from the artwork itself.

Click on the image with the Paintbrush tool. A single click gives you your signature. You may want to reduce the opacity of the signature layer and use the Multiply blending mode so that it blends into the image. 🎞

Enhancing a Book Cover

Use the Cutout filter to create a special effect for a book cover—or any other project.

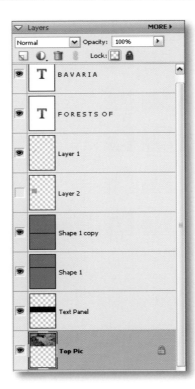

1. Create the Book Cover.

We've already created a standard book cover, with several layers in place. There are two images, each on its own layer. Additionally, two text layers and a shape layer are grouped to create the title panel. The book cover could work as it is, with two beautiful photos, but we'll add some special effects to make it stand out a bit more.

2. Apply the Cutout Filter.

Select the layer for the bottom image. Choose Filter > Filter Gallery to quickly see previews of different filters on the image. For this image, we'll use the Cutout filter. Change the settings for Levels, Edge Simplicity, and Edge Fidelity. Levels determines how many sections are created; a higher value results in more detail and complexity. Click OK to apply the filter.

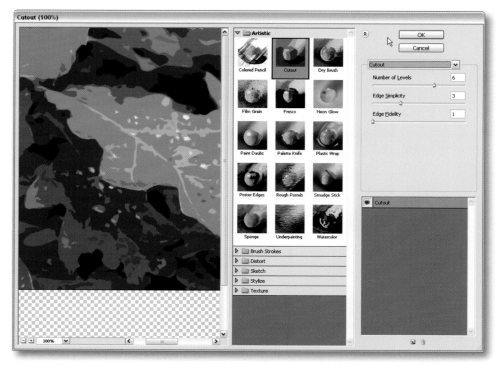

3. Apply the Same Filter to the Top Image.

To balance this book cover, we'll apply the same filter to the top image. Select the layer, and then press Ctrl+F. Photoshop Elements applies the last filter you used with the same settings.

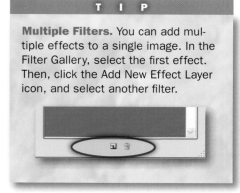

T I P

Multiple Filters. You can add multiple effects to a single image. In the Filter Gallery, select the first effect. Then, click the Add New Effect Layer icon, and select another filter.

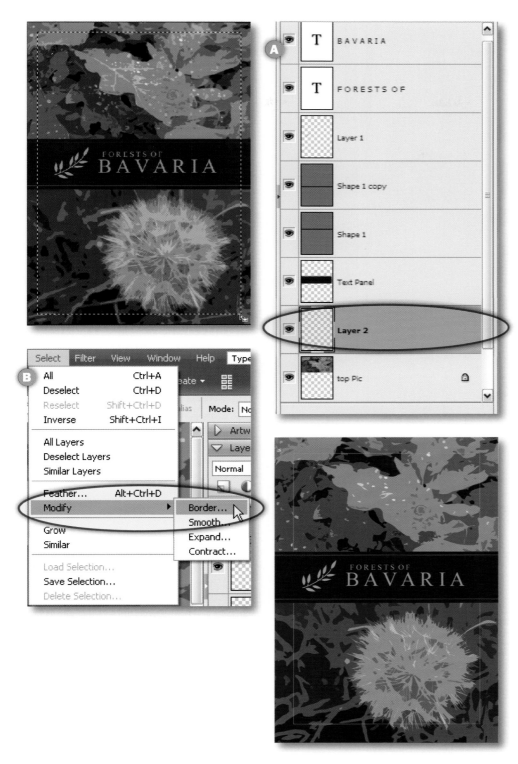

4. Add a Border.

To put the finishing touch on this cover, we'll add a border. First, create a new layer **A**. Then, select the Rectangular Marquee tool, and drag a rectangle that is even with the edge. Press the space-bar to reposition the rectangle as you draw it.

Now choose Select > Modify > Border **B**. Select 3 pixels for the width. Select a color with the Eyedropper tool; we'll use a light color from one of the images. Press Alt+Backspace to fill the border. Click outside the border to deselect the border and see the final results. ▦

Creating a Promotional Card

Show off your photographic masterpieces on a customized promotional card. Frames make it easy.

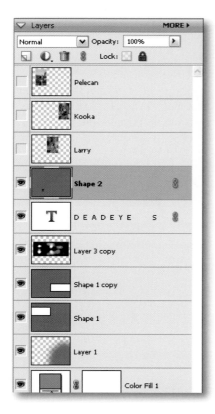

1. Create the Background.

You can use a photo card to introduce your work to clients, share images with your family, or distribute photos just about anywhere else. First, create a background to fit your purpose. In this example, we've already created several layers: a textured background, a shape, text, a color fill adjustment layer, and a blur. When you work with layers, you can easily make changes to each component. For example, you could change the color fill every time you use the card, choosing a color that complements your photos.

2. Select Your Images.

Decide which photographs you want to include on the card. Open the images in the Editor so that they appear in the Photo Bin, add them to layers in the card project, or note where the files are located on your computer so you can find them easily later.

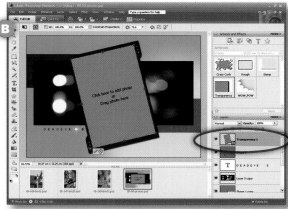

3. Add a Frame.

In the Artwork and Effects palette, choose Frames from the pop-down menu. Photoshop Elements includes dozens of frames you can choose from, organized by category. The How To Wow with Photoshop 5.0 CD also includes frames, and if you've copied them to your hard drive, they'll appear in the category called How To Wow Frames **A**.

Select a frame, and drag it onto the background. We're using the transparency frame from the How to Wow CD, but all the frames work the same way. When you drag the frame onto the background, it appears on a new layer **B**. You can resize it by dragging a corner. To rotate it, move the mouse just outside the border until you see the curved double-arrow, and then drag in the direction you want to rotate. When it's in position, click the check mark to commit **C**.

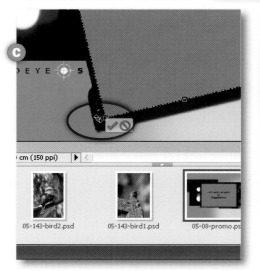

4. Place an Image.

There are several ways to put an image into a frame. If you click in the frame, Photoshop Elements will prompt you to browse to the image you want to include; when you select it, it appears in the frame. Or, you can drag the image from the Photo Bin or from a layer and drop it into the frame. However you bring the image in, it's automatically rotated and resized to fit into the frame.

To enlarge the image, move the slider at the top to the right. Only the part of the image that is within the frame shows. You can also rotate the image 90, 180, or 270 degrees by clicking the rotation symbol repeatedly. When the image is the correct size and at the appropriate angle, click the check mark to commit.

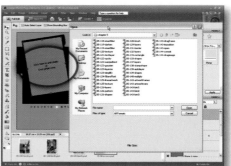

T I P

Layer Order Is Important. Pay attention to the order of layers in the Layers palette. How they're arranged makes all the difference in the effect that layer styles, adjustment layers, and blending modes have on your project.

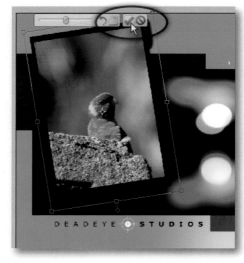

5. Add More Frames.

You can add as many frames as you like, and they can be different sizes, rotated at different angles. Just drag each frame onto the project, resize and rotate it, commit, and then add a photo.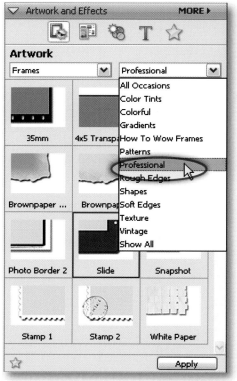

Multipage projects

You aren't limited to a single page. In fact, you can quickly use an existing page as a template. Or start from scratch on a new page.

Adding a Page with the Same Layout

Create the first page to serve as a template for all the pages in your project. You may want to use a background and frames, add shapes or graphics, or choose from the themes included with Photoshop Elements. You can even include photographs, applying filters to fade them into the background or using a photo to serve as a logo on a page.

To add a duplicate page, choose Edit > Add Page with Current Layout. A new page opens, with the same layout elements, ready for you to add new images. Any photo that is not attached to a frame—either a frame you added or a frame that is part of a theme—is considered part of the layout. If you are arranging photos without using frames, add pages before you place the photos.

The saved page appears in the Photo Bin, and you can flip through all the pages in your project to see them.

Adding a Blank Page

If you want each page in your creation to have a different look, add blank pages, and start anew each time. When the first page is done, choose Edit > Add Blank Page. A new blank page will open. The saved first page appears in the Photo Bin.

T I P

Partial Pages. If you want to use part of a layout for every page, go ahead and add a page with the same layout. Then, on the new page, delete the layers you don't want to include. You can even replace the image on the background layer.

Saving the Creation

Multiple-page projects must be saved in Photo Creations Format (PSE). When you save the project in PSE format, you can create and print up to 30 pages at one time, without having to open and edit each image separately.

To view your creation, double-click it in the Organizer, and then scroll through the pages. 🖩

Mapping Your Photos

Share your travel photos by creating a map that shows where the images were taken.

1. Collect Your Photos.

Creating a map gallery is a great way to document travel experiences. Photoshop Elements saves map galleries in Flash format so they're easy to share on the Web. To begin, import your images into the Organizer, and then create a collection for the images you want to include in your map. Display the collection.

We've gathered photos from our travels, which we'll be placing on a map of Australia.

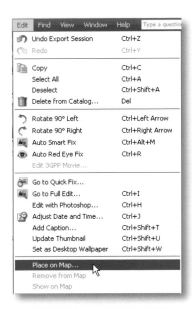

2. Open the Map.

Select an image in the collection. Choose Edit > Place on Map. Type a map location, and then click Find. For example, we'll type "Australia" to display the entire country. If you are documenting travel through specific neighborhoods of a city, you might want a tighter focus, such as the city name. A map appears on the lefthand side, with a red pushpin centered in the area you specified.

You can zoom in and out to see more detail or to see a greater area on the map. The map is a Yahoo map; you can show the road map, a satellite image of the area, or both (hybrid).

3. Place Images on the Map.

Drag the images onto the map, corresponding with their geographical area. Photoshop Elements adds a pushpin to each area to indicate an image. Click on a pin with the Hand tool to see a thumbnail of the image. If more than one image has been placed at a location, you can scroll through the images.

T I P

Mapping Tags. To map all the images with a particular tag to the same location on the map, right-click the tag, and choose Place On Map. Type the location for the image and click Find. Then click OK in the Look Up Address dialog box to confirm the location.

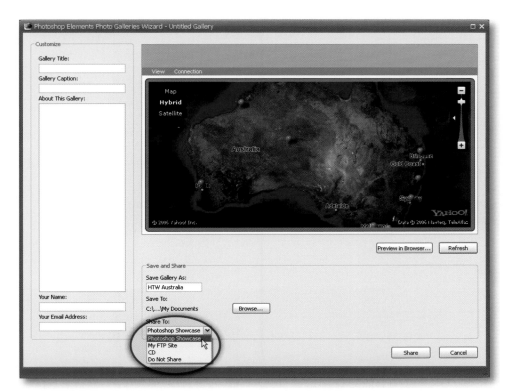

4. Create a Gallery to Share.

To create a project that you can share with others, click Share in the Map area. Then click Share in the dialog box to accept the Yahoo agreement. Next, in the Photoshop Elements Photo Galleries wizard, give the gallery a title and a caption, and write a brief description of the photo collection. You can also include your name and email address at the bottom.

Specify a file name and location for the gallery. You can share it on your own FTP site, a CD, or the Photoshop Showcase, an online service included with Photoshop Elements. Click Share. 🏛

Making Stamps

Commemorate a vacation or special event with a customized stamp.

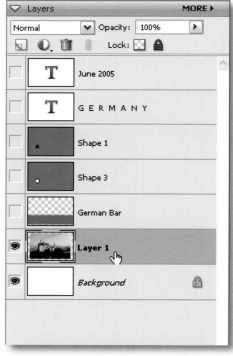

1. Prepare the Photograph.

Select the photograph you want to use for your commemorative stamp. Land-scape images work well. Edit the image in Photoshop Elements to enhance the image. Then, add other elements you want to include in the stamp. For exam-ple, we've added a colored bar across the bottom, a text layer that identifies the country, a text layer that identifies the date, and shapes that provide a regal touch.

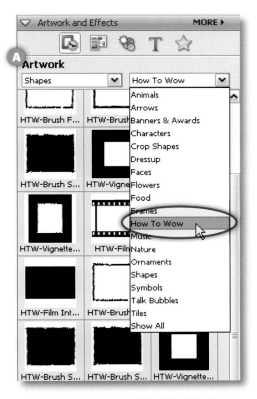

2. Create the Stamp Edge.

To create the appearance of a postage stamp, we need to add a traditional scalloped edge. We've included a stamp edge shape in the How to Wow presets. Select the Artwork and Effects Panel **A**, and then choose the HTW-stamp shape from the Shape menu. (If the HTW-stamp shape isn't listed, choose HTW-Elements shapes from the drop-down menu.)

Drag and drop the stamp shape on to the document window to get the Defined Size **B** to match the size of our sample project. Photoshop Elements creates a new layer for the shape; name it "Stamp edge." If you wish to resize your stamp simply click and drag from the corner handles. Then click the Commit button to continue.

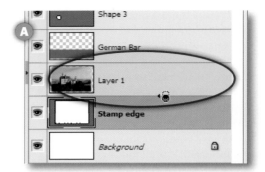

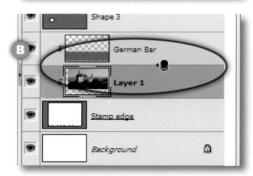

3. Group the Layers.

At the moment, the stamp edge is filled with a solid color, obscuring the image. Move the Stamp edge layer to the bottom of the layer stack in the Layers palette, just above the Background layer. Now, we need to use the Stamp edge layer as a clipping mask. Press the Alt key and click the line between the Stamp edge layer **A** and the image layer, and then Alt-click between the image layer and the layer that contains the colored bar **B** or any other shapes you've created that extend beyond the stamp edge.

After you've clipped the layers, you may need to reposition the image, the text, or another object. To reposition a layer, select it and then use the Move tool.

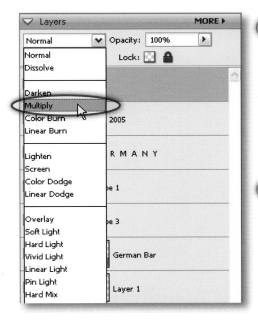

4. Add a Seal.

We'll add a seal that looks like a post-mark to add authenticity to this stamp. You can scan in a seal you drew your-self, or create one in a drawing applica-tion. Open the seal file in Photoshop Elements, so that you can see it and the stamp at the same time. Drag the seal onto the stamp file **A**; Photoshop Ele-ments creates a new layer for it.

Our seal has a white background that blocks out the image. To correct that, we'll use one of the darkening blend-ing modes, which have a neutral color of white. The Multiply blending mode works well **B**. The white background disappears, and the seal looks more realistic. You may want to reduce the opacity of the seal as well to make it fainter. ▥

WR

T I P

Add Seals to Multiple Stamps. If you're creating several stamps, you can add the same seal to them quick-ly. Add the seal to the first stamp, as we've done here. When you've applied the blending mode and adjusted the opacity, drag the seal layer from the first stamp onto the next. All the layer properties travel with it; just position the seal where you want it.

6

CREATIVE PRESENTATION

Enticing Viewers with a Variety of Formats

WE'VE RETOUCHED, color-corrected, enhanced, optimized, and tickled our images until they can stand it no longer. If a picture says a thousand words, ours would simply be yelling MERCY over and over again. It's time to put them out of their misery and do something with them. We'll set them loose on the world in the form of creative presentations.

Let's Be Nerds Together

You might think that authoring your own VCD or DVD would be a difficult thing. Or perhaps you've always assumed that creating a Web site photo gallery is best left to the nerds. In that case, we'll all be nerds. It's easy to be a nerd if you read this chapter.

We'll hold your hand as you turn those lovely photos of your niece's wedding into a slide show, complete with narration, that all the relatives can watch at home using their DVD players. And we'll be there with you as you convert your portfolio of client projects to a Web gallery for potential clients to view.

Okay, you don't actually have to be a nerd to do these things. But we should warn you that your image is likely to change. When you send personalized greeting cards, bound photo books, and panoramic images to others, they'll start to talk. Before long, relatives will be asking you to program their VCRs, asking you how their cell phones work, and giving you pocket protectors as gifts.

Feeding the Frenzy

A few of our friends have fallen into a new cult, and quite frankly, we're frightened. We're speaking, of course, about scrapbookers. Otherwise sensible people gather all manner of things and stick, cut, staple, paste, and fold them into books. Well, we're jumping on that bandwagon, but we're taking Photoshop Elements along for the ride. We think creating digital scrapbook pages can satisfy scrapbookers' cravings while keeping these gentle souls safe from

glue fumes and staplers. In fact, we're so excited about digital scrapbook pages that we'll even show you the secret scrapbooker's handshake.

Print It

The digital world is amazing, as we've seen throughout this book. But we suspect that, at some point, you'll want to print something. Whether it's for your great-aunt Susie or the living room wall, there remains a certain satisfaction in looking at a printed photograph.

With Photoshop Elements, you can not only make sure your images are in great shape before you print, but you can keep from wasting paper as well. Picture packages help you assemble multiple photographs on a single sheet of paper, arranged to fit as efficiently as possible.

To help you find the images you're looking for, we recommend printing contact sheets (to a printer, or, if you have Acrobat, to a PDF file) that give you a quick visual index of the images in a folder or collection.

Creating a PDF Slide Show

Combine photos of different dimensions in a PDF slide show to share with friends and family. Anyone can view your slide show using the free Adobe Reader.

1. Prepare Your Images.

In the Organizer, select the images you want to include in the slide show. They needn't all be the same size, or even the same orientation (wide or tall). A PDF slide show can display images of a different sizes, even in a full-screen slide show.

We recommend saving the images you want to include in the project into a new collection: In the Collections tab, choose New > New Collection. Name the collection, and then drag the images you want to use in the slide show into that collection. Collections are an excellent way to organize your images.

T I P

Viewing PDF Files. To enjoy your PDF slide show, a viewer needs to have either Adobe Acrobat or Adobe Reader. Adobe Reader is available free—for Windows, Mac OS, and other platforms—from Adobe's Web site at http://www.adobe.com.

2. Open the Creation Wizard.

Select the images in your collection, and then click the Create Menu. In the Create menu select Slide Show and click OK.

You won't see PDF slide show listed in the Creation Setup dialog box. We'll choose the PDF format after we've designed the slide show.

3. Set Slide Show Preferences.

In the Slide Show Preferences dialog box, set duration, transition, and other information for the entire slide show. Duration determines how long the slide appears on screen. Transition determines how one slide leaves the screen and another appears. Transition Duration determines how long that transition takes. As you change settings, the preview window shows you how transitions will look. (Some transitions, such as Clock Wipe, are not supported in a PDF file and are converted to Fade transitions instead.)

You can also set a background color to provide a consistent look and feel to your slide show, and you can include the text and audio captions that you've already created. If you want to fill the screen with your image every time, select a Crop To Fit Slide option. The Pan and Zoom feature does not work with a PDF slide show, nor does the Repeat Soundtrack option. Click OK to continue.

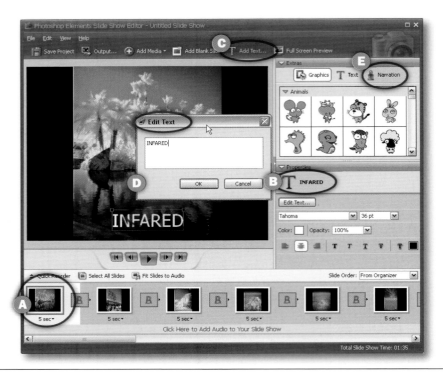

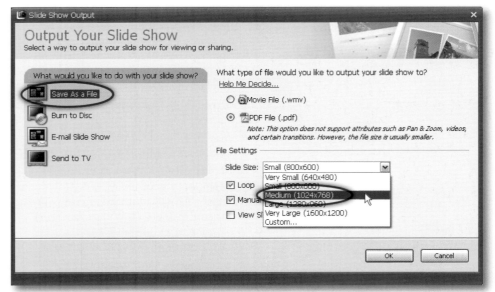

4. Customize Each Slide.

In the Slide Show Editor, you can customize the caption, duration, and transition for each slide. Select a slide from the filmstrip at the bottom of the window **A**, and then make changes in the Properties section **B**. To change the slide order, rearrange the thumbnails in the filmstrip.

To add a caption to the text, click the Add Text button **C** and type the text, or double-click a text style in the Extras section and then type your text. To edit an existing caption, double-click it and then type new text **D**. You can drag the caption box anywhere on the slide. To add an audio caption, click Narration in the Extras section **E**, and then record the caption.

5. Save the Slide Show.

Click the Output button at the top of the Slide Show Editor. In the Slide Show Output dialog box, select Save As A File, and then select PDF File. Choose a slide size; if you expect viewers to open the slide show on a handheld device, choose a small size; if they'll be displaying the slide show on a large screen, choose a larger size. Select Loop if you want the slide show to play continuously. Select Manual Advance to prevent the slides from advancing automatically; if this option is selected, the viewer will need to press the keyboard to move to each new slide. Select View Slide Show After Saving to open the slide show in Acrobat or Adobe Reader and view it.

Click OK to save the file. Name the file and select a location for it on your hard drive. If you chose to preview the file, it will open in Acrobat or Adobe Reader. ▦

Making a Multimedia Presentation

Photos, audio files, and text captions all come together in a multimedia file you can save as a movie or burn to a VCD or DVD.

1. Prepare the Images.

In the Organizer, add text captions and audio captions to files you want to include in your multimedia presentation. If any images need touch-ups, open them in the Editor, make the necessary changes, and then save the new files.

2. Create a Slide Show.

Select the images in the Organizer, and then click the Create menu. In the Create menu, select Slide Show. You'll see the same options that appear when you create a PDF slide show, but some of them have different effects in movies than in PDF files.

In the Slide Show Preferences dialog box, select options to apply to the entire slide show, including the default slide duration and transition. Select Include Photo Captions As Text to use the captions you've already created. If you have audio captions as well, select Include Audio Captions As Narration. To pan each image and then zoom into it, select Apply Pan And Zoom To All Slides. If you want to play a background soundtrack repeatedly during the slide show, select Repeat Soundtrack Until Last Slide. Click OK to continue.

3. Customize the Slides.

Select a slide from the filmstrip at the bottom of the Slide Show Editor to make changes to it **A**. To change a slide's duration, select its thumbnail and then specify a new duration in the Properties section **B**. If an audio file is attached to the slide, Photoshop Elements automatically lengthens the duration to include the entire audio file. To change the length or type of a transition, click the transition in the filmstrip, and then change the transition type or duration in the Properties section.

To change text in a caption, click the text and then click Edit Text in the Properties section. You can also drag the text box to reposition it. To create a new text box, click Add Text and then type a caption. To create a new audio caption, click Narration in the Extras section and then record the audio.

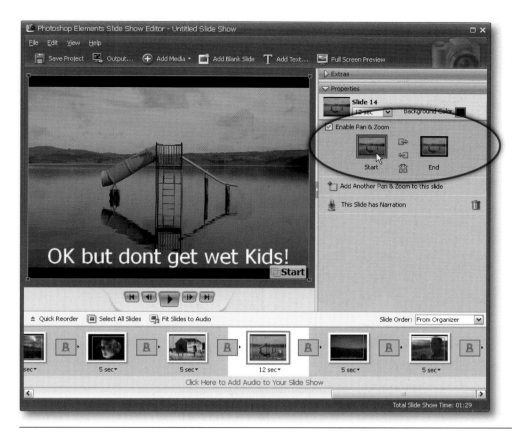

4. Adjust the Pan & Zoom Settings.

If you've enabled Pan & Zoom for the slide show, you can customize the way the slide show zooms into each image. The green rectangle indicates how much of the image is displayed initially, and the red rectangle indicates the part that shows just before the image changes. To adjust the start image, click the Start thumbnail and then reposition the green rectangle in the preview window; to adjust the end image, click the End thumbnail and reposition the red rectangle. To remove the pan and zoom from a slide, deselect Enable Pan & Zoom.

5. Add Background Music.

To play a music file in the background of your slide show, choose Add Media > Audio From Organizer or Audio From Folder. If you choose an audio file from the Organizer, click Play to preview it. Select the music file you want to use, and then click OK or Open.

T I P

Recording Audio Captions. We recommend recording audio captions for images in the Organizer, rather than in the Creation Wizard. If you record a caption in the wizard, it's only available in that slide show. If you create it in the Organizer, the audio file is attached to the image so that you can use it in future projects.

6. Preview the Project.

Click the Save Project button, and give the project a name. You'll be able to find it in the Organizer later to make changes to it. To preview the slide show, click the Play button under the preview window. You can get a sense of whether your music, caption, duration, and transition choices work the way you expected them to be. The preview is often a little jerkier than the final movie, so don't be concerned if it's not perfectly smooth. Make any changes you need to make, and preview the movie again.

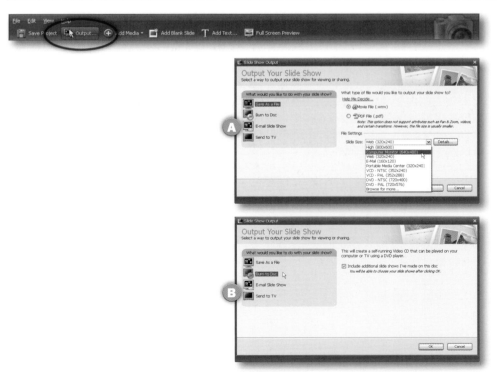

7. Output the Project.

When you're satisfied with the slide show settings, click the Output button. You can save the project as a movie file **A**, burn it to a VCD or DVD **B**, view it on your TV, or share it online. Saving it as a movie file gives you the most flexibility; you can always burn a movie file to disc, send it to your TV, or share it with others later. 🖮

Creating a Greeting Card

Personalize an occasion with a custom greeting card from your own photo collection. You can print your own or have it professionally printed.

HELLO FROM
WOODSIDE
VICTORIA

FROM MIKE, WAYNE
AND JACK.

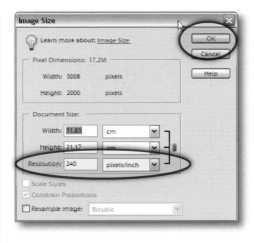

1. Prepare Your Photos.

Select the photo or photos you want to use on your greeting card, and touch them up in the Editor. Clean up any blemishes, correct color problems, remove power lines, or do anything else you need to do to make the image more appealing.

If you'll be printing the card or having it professionally printed, make sure the image resolution is high enough to print well. Choose Image > Resize > Image Size, and check the Resolution value in the Document Size section of the dialog box. A value of 240 dpi or higher is fine for most printing. If the resolution is too low, deselect Resample Image and type a higher resolution value. Photoshop Elements will resize the image at the new resolution; the default image width and height will be smaller at the higher resolution.

Save any changes you've made to the image.

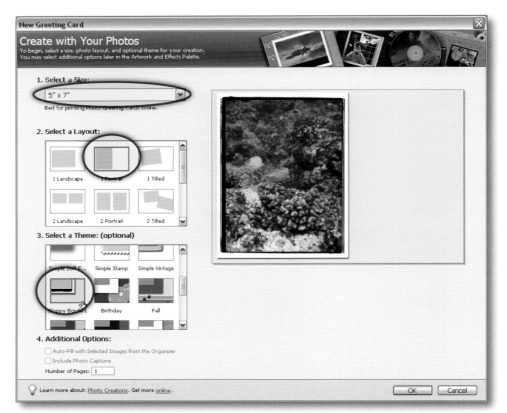

2. Select a Card Layout.

In the Organizer, select the image or images you want to use in the card. Then, choose Create > Greeting Card. The New Greeting Card wizard opens.

Select a card size: 4"x 6", 5"x7", or A6 (105 mm x 148 mm). The best size for professional printing is 5"x7". Then, select a layout that's appropriate for the orientation and number of your photos. For example, if you're using two portrait (or tall) images, you might select 2 Portrait or, for a more whimsical card, 2 Tilted. Each of the layouts creates a single-sided card.

Next, select a theme if you want one. Many of the themes use frames that are available in the Editor. When you select a theme, the preview window uses a placeholder image to show the appearance of a card with that theme. You can select one as a starting point; you'll be able to customize it further in a moment.

INSIGHT

Get the Latest Templates.

Adobe introduces new templates for Photoshop Elements creations frequently. Update your templates occasionally to make sure you have the full range of templates available. Choose Edit > Preferences > Services. Then click Update Creations. If you're connected to the Internet, Photoshop Elements checks for new templates and downloads them onto your computer.

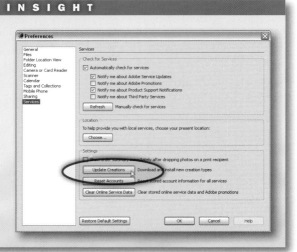

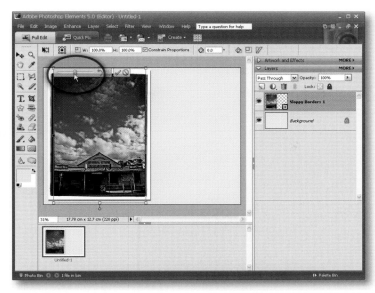

3. Customize Your Card.

Click OK in the New Greeting Card dialog box. Your card opens in the Editor, so you can make adjustments to it. The border in the theme is a frame on a layer, so you can edit it as you would any other frame: select it and then resize it or change the width; as you change the border, the image resizes to fit it. To change the scale of the image itself, double-click it and move its slider.

If you're planning to print the card to your own printer or distribute it electronically, add text in the Editor. However, if you're planning to order printed cards online, you can wait and add text then.

4. Save and Print the Card.

Choose File > Save As to save the card with any changes you've made. Select Include in the Organizer, and save the file as a PSD file. To print the card directly to your printer, choose File > Print. To order professionally printed cards online, click the triangle next to the Print or Order icon at the top of the window, and then choose Order Photo Greeting Card.

The Order Photo Greeting Cards wizard displays your draft; click Next Step to continue. Now you can adjust the card design, easily adding text. There are two text boxes. To add text, double-click in a text box, and then type the text. You can change the font, text size, or color. You can also drag the text boxes anywhere you want them to appear. When you've finished the card, click Done. A PDF file is published, and then, if you're connected to the Internet, you can order your cards online.

Scrapbook Pages

Assemble digital scrapbook pages to capture memories through photos, ticket stubs, passport stamps, and more. You can be just as creative with a digital scrapbook as with a physical one—with less mess.

Assembling Contents

Plan your scrapbook pages before you begin working in Photoshop Elements. Gather the items you want to memorialize: photographs, hair ribbons, medals, ticket stubs, passport stamps, love letters, dried flowers, valentines, campaign buttons, or anything else that is meaningful to you or the person you're creating the scrapbook for.

Then, think of the items that might add depth and interest to the scrapbook page, or that might help set a mood. For example, you can scan in decorative thumbtacks to provide a three-dimensional feel, or use confetti to add a celebratory mood. Or scan photo corners to tuck at the edges of photos to provide a nostalgic feeling. Use leaves to represent autumn, paper snowflakes for winter, or ferns for a camping trip. Be creative!

Scan all the items into Photoshop Elements. Scanner options vary, but you'll get the best results if you scan items in with a resolution of 300 dpi. Most scanners also let you specify that you're scanning text for better results with letters, diplomas, or other text-heavy material.

If you restore images using Photoshop Elements, save a version of each image with the layers flattened so that it will be easier to work with in the scrapbook pages.

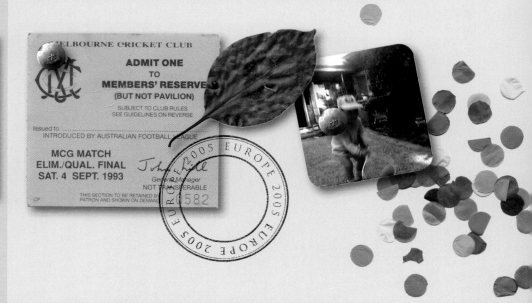

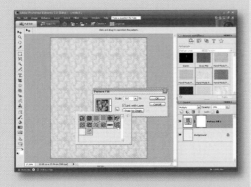

Creating the Background

If you're creating multiple scrapbook pages, you probably want them to have the same look and feel. A consistent background can set the tone for the pages.

Create a letter-size page in Photoshop Elements, with a resolution that is appropriate for your intended use. If you think you may want to print the scrapbook pages someday, use a 300 dpi resolution. Higher resolutions give you more flexibility; it's easier to remove information from a file than to add it later.

To add a texture to the background, click the Add Adjustment Layer icon, and then choose Pattern. In the Pattern Fill dialog box, click the pattern thumbnail and then choose the pattern you want to use. We've included many patterns on the How to Wow DVD. You can scale the texture of any pattern you choose; experiment to see what you like best. Click OK to apply the pattern. Reduce the opacity of the adjustment layer so that you can read any text you add to it.

This page will serve as the template for all your scrapbook pages. If you want text to appear on each page (such as a header or footer), add it to this template page. Add any other elements that you want to have on every page, and then choose File > Save As. Save the page as a Photoshop file (.psd) and name it "Scrapbook template." Choose File > Save As again, and save the file with a new name for the first page you're creating. Each time you create a new page, open the Scrapbook Template file and choose File > Save As to save the new page with a unique name.

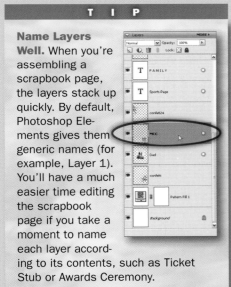

TIP

Name Layers Well. When you're assembling a scrapbook page, the layers stack up quickly. By default, Photoshop Elements gives them generic names (for example, Layer 1). You'll have a much easier time editing the scrapbook page if you take a moment to name each layer according to its contents, such as Ticket Stub or Awards Ceremony.

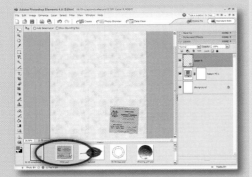

Adding Elements to the Page

Open the scanned images you want to add to the scrapbook page in the Editor. To add an element to the page, select the image in the Photo Bin, press Ctrl+A to select the entire image, press Ctrl+C to copy it, and then return to the scrapbook page and press Ctrl+V. Photoshop Elements creates a new layer for the object.

Alternatively, you can tile the images so that you see them all at once. Click the Automatically Tile Windows icon in the top-right corner of the Editor. Then, simply drag an object onto the scrapbook page and drop it there.

To add text, select the Horizontal Type tool. Then, click an insertion point and start typing, or drag a text box and start typing. You can change the font, type size, and other type attributes in the Options bar. Photoshop Elements creates a new layer for the text.

Positioning Elements

The art of scrapbooking is in the arrangement of elements on a page. You can drag elements to new locations on the page, resize them, rotate them, and change the stacking order to achieve overlapping effects.

To resize an object, select its layer and then drag the corner handles; be sure to press the Shift key as you drag to resize it proportionally.

To rotate an object, select its layer and then drag the cursor away from the object until the curved arrow appears. Then, move the cursor in the direction you want to rotate the object. Click the Commit icon or double-click the object to apply the rotation.

To change the stacking order, drag layers into new positions in the Layers palette. The bottom layer is furthest back, the top layer in the palette is the topmost layer on the page, etc.

Adding Drop Shadows

To give objects a stronger relationship to the page, and to add a three-dimensional feel to your scrapbook, add drop shadows to objects on the page: Select the layer and then open the Styles and Effects palette. Choose Layer Styles and Drop Shadows from the menus at the top of the palette. Then choose a drop shadow style; we prefer Soft Edge for most scrapbook pages.

To change the shadow settings, double-click the layer style icon for the layer in the Layers palette. In the Style Settings dialog box, you can change the lighting angle and the shadow distance.

INSIGHT

Extracting Objects from a Background. We scanned confetti on a flatbed scanner and the result was an image of confetti on a white background. To keep the confetti, but lose the background, we'll use the Magic Extractor. Choose Image > Magic Extractor. In the Magic Extractor dialog box, use the Foreground Brush to mark the object you want to keep and the Background Brush to mark areas to exclude. Then click Preview to see how it looks. Use the Defringe option, the Add To Selection tool, and the Remove From Selection tool to touch up the selection.

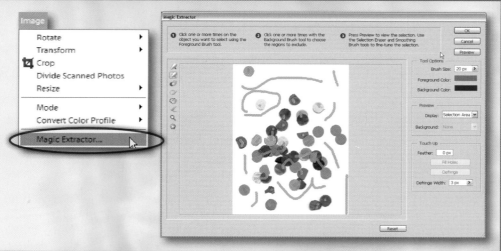

Creating a Web Gallery

Share your photos in an image gallery on the Web. You can choose from different styles to fit your photos and your audience.

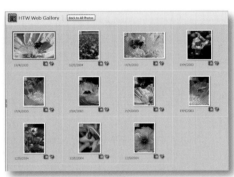

1. Prepare the Images.

Make any adjustments to the images you want to include in your gallery in the Editor. You can also add captions in the Organizer to appear with the images online.

2. Choose a Gallery Style.

Select the images you want to include in the gallery. Click Create. Select HTML Photo Gallery, and click OK. In the Adobe HTML Photo Gallery dialog box, select a gallery style. Each gallery style has a different look and feel; some include filmstrip-style navigation, which can make it easier for viewers to enjoy your images.

3. Customize the Gallery.

After you've selected a gallery style, customize it. In the Customize Panel, type a title for your gallery **A**. If you want to include contact information, type your email address for the banner. In the Thumbnails tab **B**, optimize your gallery to suit different Internet connection speeds. Customize the appearance of the gallery by customizing the backgound colors for the main window, the thumbnails, and the slide show **C**.

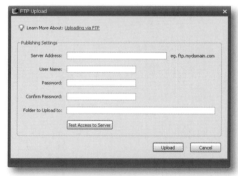

4. Save and Share Your Gallery.

Type a name for the site folder for the gallery files. By default, Photoshop Elements saves the site folder in the My Documents folder. To change the destination folder, click Browse and navigate to the folder you want to use.

Click Share to create the gallery and to preview it. Photoshop Elements creates three subfolders in the site folder: Images, Pages, and Thumbnails.

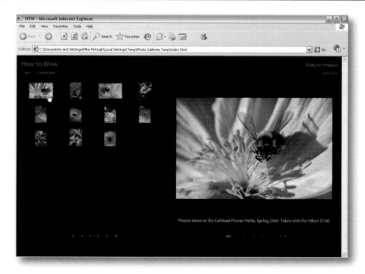

5. Copy the Files to the Web.

Copy the contents of the site folder to your Web server. Make sure the contents remain in the appropriate subfolders. For help transferring the files, contact your Internet service provider.

Creating a Flash Gallery

Present your images in an interactive Flash gallery, which you can share with the world.

1. Start the Wizard.

To create a photo gallery, first select the images you want to use in the Organizer. It's easiest if you create a collection for them or tag them for your project. When the images are selected, choose Photo Galleries from the Create menu. The Photoshop Elements Photo Galleries wizard opens. The images you selected are displayed, in order, on the left side of the dialog box.

2. Set Up a Gallery.

The wizard can help you set up different kinds of galleries. For starters, you can choose to create a Web gallery (in HTML format), an animated gallery, or an interactive gallery. Choose each option to see samples of the galleries. We'll choose Interactive.

Next, select a style of interactive gallery. Click each thumbnail to see a description and preview. We like the slides, but you can choose any style. Click Next Step.

3. Customize the Gallery.

Give the gallery a title. You can also add a subtitle and your email address, if you like. Depending on the Web gallery style you chose, you may be able to enable sound effects, display captions, or apply an old paper effect as well.

To see how your gallery will appear, click Refresh. The preview screen shows the gallery as viewers will see it. For an even more accurate look, click Preview in Browser.

4. Share the Gallery.

We're ready to share this gallery with friends, family, and maybe the general public. Type a name for the gallery. By default, Photoshop Elements saves it to the My Documents folder; click Browse if you want to navigate to a different location. Then, choose where you want to share the gallery. You can upload it to your own FTP site, burn it to a CD, or use the free Adobe Photoshop Showcase. We'll use the Photoshop Showcase. Click Share to continue.

Photoshop Elements creates the gallery. If you're using Photoshop Showcase for the first time, you'll need to register; if you already have a free account, it will welcome you. Click Yes to share the gallery, and then click Next. You can invite friends and, if you want to, share it with the public. Click Next again, and Photoshop Showcase uploads the gallery.

Click Done in Photoshop Elements. The gallery is available in the Organizer. ▥

INSIGHT

Sharing Individual Photos. You can use Photoshop Showcase to share photos without creating snazzy galleries, as well. In the Organizer, select the images you want to share. Then, click the Share icon, and choose Share with Adobe Photoshop Showcase > Share Photos.

Creating a Flipbook

Catch the action by animating a set of photos in a flipbook that you can share with others.

1. Take a Sequence of Photographs.

A flipbook is a simple form of animation, in which each image serves as a frame in a sequence. When you flip through the book, the image appears to move. You can create digital flipbooks using Photoshop Elements. Take several photos of an event as it unfolds; the more frequently you take photos, the smoother the animation will appear. For best results, use a tripod or other tool to keep the camera steady so that the images will align properly as they flip. For our flipbook, Jack Davis used a tripod to take about 60 photos of someone writing "Happy Birthday" in sand on a beach.

2. Import the Photos.

In the Organizer, choose File > Get Photos > From Camera or Card Reader. Import the images into the Organizer window. Then, to find them easily, create a collection for those images. Display the collection, and rearrange the images, if necessary, to put them in the order in which you want them to appear in the flipbook.

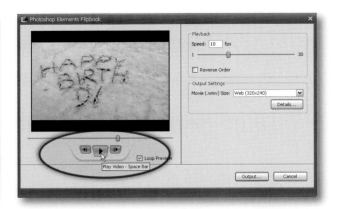

3. Open the Flipbook Wizard.

Select all the images in the collection. Click the arrow next to create, and choose Flipbook from the menu. The selected images are included in the order in which they appear in the Organizer, with the first image in the preview window. To preview the flipbook, click the Play button beneath the preview window. You can pause and advance or move backward one frame at a time by pressing the other playback buttons.

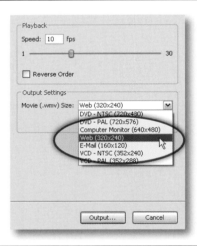

4. Adjust Settings for the Flipbook.

By default, the flipbook displays 15 frames per second, but that's a pretty fast pace. Experiment with different frame rates for the best results.

Choose an output setting profile from the Output Settings menu. Photoshop Elements will save the file as a .wmv file, but different profiles result in higher or lower movie quality and larger or smaller file sizes. For information about the settings of a particular profile and when to use it, choose the profile and click Details.

5. Output the Flipbook.

Click Output to save the flipbook. Name the flipbook and choose a location for it. Click Save. That's all there is to it. When Photoshop Elements has finished creating the flipbook, it appears in the Photo Browser with a flipbook icon that looks like a piece of filmstrip. To play the flipbook, double-click it in the Organizer.

You can burn a flipbook to a CD or VCD, import it into Premiere Elements, or export it to a mobile phone. ▥

Producing a Panorama

Give a breathtaking scene its due! Use Photoshop Elements to merge multiple photos for a panoramic effect.

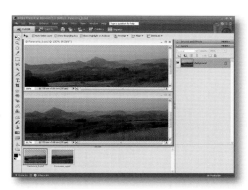

1. Take the Photos.

As you take the photographs, try to keep the images aligned. This is the time to take advantage of that tripod you were given for your birthday! If you don't have a tripod, keep in mind that the images will merge together more gracefully if the camera angle and height are consistent.

Load the images into Organizer, and then open them in the Editor.

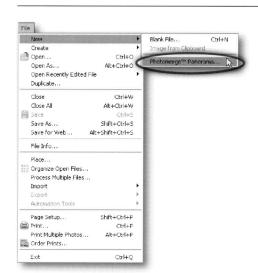

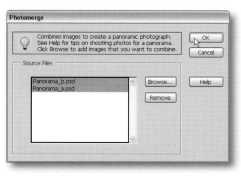

2. Use Photomerge.

Choose File > New > Photomerge Panorama. This command can be tricky to find, but it's in the New submenu because you're creating a new image from the ones you're combining.

In the Photomerge dialog box, verify that the correct images appear. If you need to add any images, click Browse and navigate to them. When all the images for your panorama are in the dialog box, click OK. Photoshop Elements merges the images, attempting to align them.

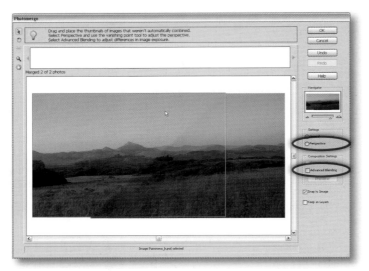

3. Make Adjustments, as Necessary.

Photoshop Elements does a pretty good job of merging the elements, but you may end up with a seam, or with a significant color difference between one side of the image and the other. Click Advanced Blending to let Photoshop Elements attempt to correct such problems, and then click Preview to see how well it has done.

If the perspective is off, click Perspective. You can also use the rotation tool to nudge an image into place.

4. Save the Image.

When you're happy with the image, click OK. Photoshop Elements creates a new file with the images stitched together. You may want to crop the image, if the originals weren't perfectly aligned. You can make any other changes to the image, as well, treating this image as you would any other image in Photoshop Elements.

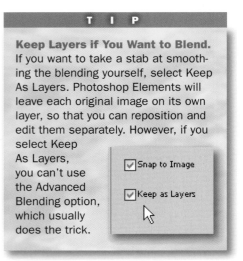

T I P

Keep Layers if You Want to Blend.
If you want to take a stab at smoothing the blending yourself, select Keep As Layers. Photoshop Elements will leave each original image on its own layer, so that you can reposition and edit them separately. However, if you select Keep As Layers, you can't use the Advanced Blending option, which usually does the trick.

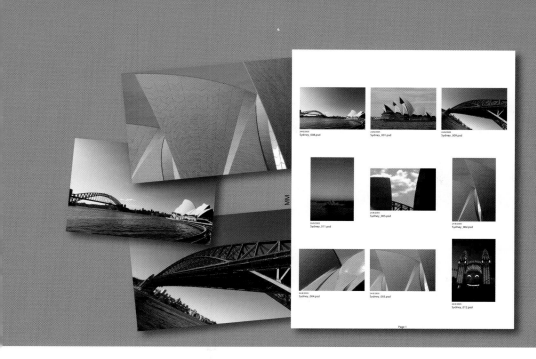

Making a Contact Sheet

Create an index of the photos in a collection, on a CD, or in a folder. A contact sheet of image thumbnails helps you find images quickly.

1. Select the Photos.

In the Organizer, select the images you want to include in the contact sheet. Usually, you'd want to include all the images in a collection, or on a CD, or in a specific folder. You can also create a contact sheet from the Editor if the images are open in the Photo Bin.

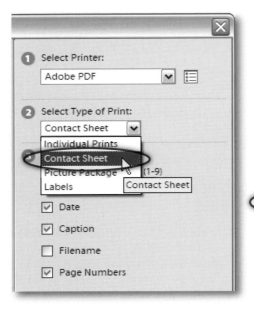

2. Prepare the Contact Sheet.

Choose File > Print. Select your printer, and then choose Contact Sheet as the type of print. Specify the number of columns per page, which determines how big the thumbnails are. The default page size is shown beneath the preview window; to change the page size, click Page Setup and choose a different paper size. You can also change the paper orientation.

You can choose to print the date, caption, and file name for each image. If you're printing enough images that they'll require multiple pages, you can also print page numbers on each page. If you're working with color management, click More Options to choose a print space appropriate for your printer.

3. Print the Contact Sheet.

Click Print. Photoshop Elements prints the contact sheet to your printer, using the settings you specified. If you have Adobe Acrobat, you can choose to print to the PDF printer instead, which would print the contact sheet to a PDF file. To print to a PDF, choose the PDF Printer as the printer. 🖮

Producing a Picture Package

Print sets of photos in standard sizes, just like the ones you receive from photography studios.

1. Open Images in Editor.

Most of us print on standard sheets of paper, making it difficult to print standard-sized photos (4 x 6 inches, say, or 3 x 5 inches) without wasting a great deal of paper. Creating a picture package lets you print a set of photos efficiently. First, open the photo or photos you want to print in the Editor. Make sure their resolution is high enough to print well on your printer.

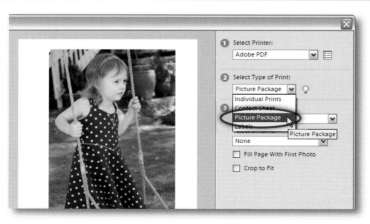

2. Select Picture Package.

Choose File > Print Multiple Photos. In the Print Photos dialog box, select your printer. Then, click Page Setup, choose the paper size and orientation, and click OK. The preview window in the Print Photos dialog box changes to reflect the settings in the Page Setup dialog box. Select Picture Package.

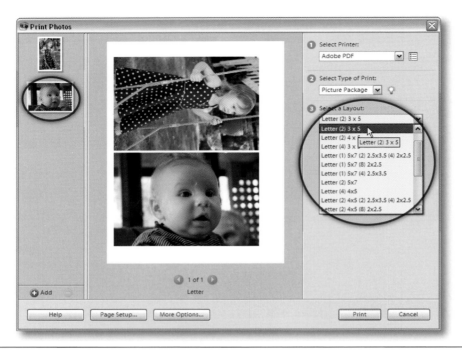

3. Customize the Layout.

Choose a layout with standard sizes for the photos. Some layouts contain copies at only one size; some contain a mixture of sizes. If you want all the photos to be identical, select Fill Page With First Photo. If you want to mix and match photos, drag them from the upper-left corner onto the page where you want them to print. For example, you can print three copies of one photo, two of a different photo, and the rest of the page in a third photo.

You can also frame the images by choosing a frame from the Select A Frame menu. For example, you could use an oval frame for images that will be displayed in oval picture frames.

4. Print.

To ensure you're printing at the quality you want, click Page Setup, and then click Properties. Make sure the settings in the Properties dialog box are set to give you high-quality prints. Options available depend on the printer you're using. When you're satisfied with the settings, click OK to close the Page Setup dialog box, and then click Print. ⌨

Index

Get Inspired by the Pros!

Learn to Work Creatively and Efficiently!

You've read the book. Now see the movies!

How to Wow with Photoshop Elements **interactive training** will guide you step by step with an emphasis on uncompromising quality, last-minute flexibility, and phenomenal speed. You'll watch lessons on incredibly useful projects from organizing your zillions of photos to creating a digital scrapbook. Whether it's optimizing your image, retouching cosmetic undesirables, reconstructing priceless heirlooms, or creating customized wrapping paper, **learn the tools and techniques that will show you How to Wow!**

Here are some of the lessons available online as Workshops-On-Demand:

ELEMENTS ESSENTIALS
- Introduction to the Organizer
- Introduction to the Edit Workspace
- Introduction to the Elements Workspace
- How to Choose Your Image Size
- Creating Basic Selections
- Layers
- Color Management
- Camera Raw

PHOTO OPTIMIZING
- Auto Crop
- Crop and Straighten
- Correcting Perspective
- Quick Fix
- Levels
- Shadow Highlight
- Color Cast Removal
- Noise Reduction
- Target Selective Color

CREATIVE PROJECTS
- Pen and Ink Watercolor
- Tattoo Additions
- Wrapping Paper
- Digital Signature
- How to Wow Presets
- Postage Stamp
- Book Cover
- Promotional Card

PHOTO ENHANCING
- Blend Modes
- Dodging and Burning
- Motion Blur
- Skin Conditioning
- Skin Smoothing
- High Contrast
- High Pass Enhancement

PHOTO RETOUCHING
- Red Eye
- Blemishes and Wrinkles
- Eyes and Teeth
- Hair Color
- Rejuvenating Old Photographs
- Body Reshape
- Replace Sky
- Remove Objects

CREATIVE PRESENTATIONS
- PDF Slideshows
- Multimedia Slideshows
- Greeting Cards
- Scrapbooks
- Web Photo Gallery
- Photomerge Panorama
- Contact Sheets & Printing
- Picture Package Printing

 software**CINEMA**®

 Peachpit Press

Watch over the shoulder of the experts.

They're just waiting for you to log on!

Mike McHugh, Wayne Rankin, and Jack Davis have assembled powerful training movies that will show you exactly how to get the most out of Photoshop Elements 5.

Learning Photoshop Elements is now as easy as getting online.
Software Cinema and Peachpit Press are pleased to introduce you to the newest and easiest way to master Elements. Using new advances in streaming media, we are able to bring you the proven, step-by-step techniques in vivid, full-resolution detail. You will learn quickly and naturally as Mike walks you through each technique as if he were right there with you. ***As part of purchasing this How to Wow book, you can experience four lessons, sampling these dynamic, interactive training movies for yourself!*** *For log-in instructions simply go to www.software-cinema.com/htw.*

Jack, Mike, and Wayne have a knack for unlocking the hidden secrets of any application—always with a practical emphasis on quality, flexibility, and speed. In this How to Wow training for Software Cinema they hold nothing back. It's all here, every trick and technique (demonstrated by Mike in real time, in full resolution, with beautiful sound) that will get your images looking their creative best. From optimizing to combining to retouching, these are techniques you will use everyday! After learning these unbelievably easy and useful methods, you'll wonder how you ever worked without them. Additionally, you get their images to work along with the videos on your computer.

NOTE: Specific tutorial movies may differ from the examples shown here.

See the previous page for more information for a discount offer on our complete set of interactive Workshops-On-Demand.

 software**CINEMA**®

Peachpit
Press